TAKE
THE
CITY

Voices of Radical Municipalism

Edited by Jason Toney

BLACK
ROSE
BOOKS

Montréal•Chicago•London

Black Rose Books No. UU414

Library and Archives Canada Cataloguing in Publication

Title: Take the city : voices of radical municipalism.

Other titles: Take the city (2021)

Names: Toney, Jason, 1993- editor.

Identifiers: Canadiana (print) 20200209116 | Canadiana (ebook) 20200209124 | ISBN 9781551647296 (hardcover) | ISBN 9781551647272 (softcover) | ISBN 9781551647319 (PDF)

Subjects: LCSH: Decentralization in government. | LCSH: Municipal government. | LCSH: Local elections. | LCSH: Social movements.

Classification: LCC JS113 .T35 2021 | DDC 320.8—dc23

Cover illustration and design by Luke Carter.

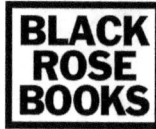

BLACK ROSE BOOKS

C.P.35788 Succ. Léo-Pariseau
Montréal, QC, H2X 0A4
Explore our books and subscribe to our newsletter:
blackrosebooks.com

Ordering Information

CANADA	USA/INTERNATIONAL	UK/IRELAND
University of Toronto Press	University of Chicago Press	Central Books
5201 Dufferin Street	Chicago Distribution Center	50 Freshwater Road
Toronto, ON	11030 South Langley Avenue	Chadwell Heath, London
M3H 5T8	Chicago, IL 60628	RM8 1RX
1-800-565-9523	(800) 621-2736 (USA)	+44 (0) 20 8525 8800
utpbooks@utpress.utoronto.ca	(773) 702-7000 (International) orders@press.uchicago.edu	contactus@centralbooks.com

Table of Contents

Acknowledgements

Gratitude is due to the contributors who shared their work and to all the hands that helped produce and refine our book. Take the City would not exist without Emanuel Guay, the initial editor, as well as Sean Devine, who volunteered to translate and edit several sections. Special recognition is also due to my partner, Ali Overing, the team at Black Rose—namely Clara-Swan Kennedy, Fawaz Halloum, and Dimitri Roussopoulos—and to the countless Montreal organizers who influenced the arch of this book.

Introduction

Jason Toney

"We have frequently printed the word Democracy. Yet I cannot too often repeat that it is a word the real gist of which still sleeps, quite unawakened, notwithstanding the resonance, and the many angry tempests out of which its syllables have come, from pen or tongue. It is a great word, whose history, I suppose, remains unwritten, because that history has yet to be enacted."

— Walt Whitman, Democratic Vistas (1871)

Roots

Radical Municipalism is an emergent global movement rooted in an enduring vision that dates back to at least ancient Athenian democracy and recalls the traditional assembly bonds of early human societies which were dismantled by the onset of hierarchical structures through industrialization, nationalism, colonialism, and the domination of capital accumulation—to name a few. While the inspirations for a municipalist approach to city politics are many (the early New England Town Meetings, the Paris Commune, Red Vienna, the works of Murray Bookchin, David Harvey, Peter Marcuse, and Abdullah Öcalan amongst others), the new municipalism is ultimately born out of a struggle against capitalism, the State, and the centralizing function of massive urbanization. The spirit of radical municipalism is visible today in places as diverse as Barcelona, Oaxaca, Hong Kong, Jackson, Mississippi, regions of Kurdistan, Detroit, Montréal, and many other cities. In the past decade, umbrella organizations like the Right to the

City Movement, Symbiosis, and Fearless Cities have carried forward the work of popular education, dual power, and confederation building alongside localized political struggles. While municipalism is concerned with decentralization and building place-based power, it also emphasizes federalism and communalism. Cooperation is the word of the day.

Throughout history, radical municipalism has gone by different names—democratic confederalism, communalism, etc.—and it has been given various qualifiers—libertarian, new, or, in our case, *radical*. The word radical is derived from the Latin *radix*, literally meaning "root." By tending to the roots of democracy, our neighbourhoods grow resilient against an all-too-common decay that permeates our cities. These many phrases do not indicate an in-fight over naming the movement. On the contrary, flourishing linguistic nuances are evidence of dynamism and they reflect the most important principles of radical municipalism.

Activist and researcher Laura Roth succinctly names and defines three core tenets of this dynamic, new municipalist movement. 1. "The feminization of politics, which stresses the dependence on reproductive activities," 2. "political ecology, emphasizing care for the natural environment," and 3. "participatory democracy, giving people a say in shaping their world through politic decision making."[1] She elaborates on feminized politics, noting that it's not merely about 'gender balance,' but rather the "transformation of power relations and their effect on the formulation of a new type of political leadership."[2] In no place in the world today is this aspect of the municipalist experiment and its impact more visible than in the autonomous region of Rojava (with a population of about 4 million) where gender equality is practiced in all decision-making bodies, beginning with the co-chairing of such bodies. This introduction explores the underlying questions of municipalism and the lessons learned from the history of the author's city, Montréal, where the lessons from the Montréal Citizens' Movement (MCM) are not well-known enough.

Why Take the City?

The question posed in the subject of this section has deliberate double meaning. First, why take the city in practice? Second, why 'Take the City' as a phrase?

1. Why take the city in practice?

According to the *2018 Revision of World Urbanization Prospects* produced by the Population Division of the UN Department of Economic and Social Affairs, 55% of the world's population lived in urban areas as of 2018 and by 2050 that number is expected to grow to 68%.[3] Activist and author Dimitri Roussopoulos refers to this trend as a "titanic shift in the history of humanity," noting that this development will have a "profound impact on all aspects of our civilisation and will determine the future of the entire planet and its ecosystems."[4] In this context, Murray Bookchin's, *Urbanization Without Cities*, framed the crossroads we face between urbanization on the one hand and citification on the other. Urbanization, for Bookchin, is associated with capital, technocracy, and centralization. Citification is linked with a long history of communalism, participatory democracy, and culture. Unhinged urbanization threatens "not only a drastic colonization of the countryside but also of the city's and the citizen's very self-identity."[5] By presenting the terms urban and city in an oppositional way helps us grasp the stakes posed by the question: why take the city?

Cities have increasingly become the heartlands of global capitalism. Financial institutions, banks, insurance companies, corporations, the real estate industry, and much else are all headquartered in cities. Financialization and speculative investment, especially on housing and land, make life for working-class people increasingly precarious. Karl Polanyi's fictitious commodities of land, labour, and money have become the foundation for these institutions that add little to no value to society, making money with money.[6] These dangerous institutions have an outsized influence on the political life of the cities in which they are based. Municipal electoral politics are all too often beholden to financial interests, rather than the interests of the people who live and work in cities. To take the city is to build new, parallel institutions to those established by the State—most notably via the establishment of citizen assemblies in neighborhoods—and to actively pressure municipal politics with radical agendas developed by coalitions of citizen

Jason Toney

groups. To do so isn't merely parochial but challenges the exact foundations on which capitalism has been established.

The ecological potential of cities is paramount. To some, it is a paradox that cities are associated with ecology, but the reason for this paradox is born out of a failure of popular education by the political left and the victory of extractivist-industry propaganda. For example, the prospect that cities can harness the efficiency of public transit, especially when free, has transformative ecological potential.[7] Urban planners and architects have developed sustainable models for building, maintaining, and restoring housing.[8] What is lacking to realize these obvious solutions to our ecological issues is not 'political will,' as it is commonly stated, but rather the lack of power of ordinary people. Here it makes sense to echo a maxim of social ecology: that our ecological crises are rooted in social issues. To tackle the issues we face in our neighbourhoods and to build power locally and confederally is a critical tool and solving the existential threat of ecological collapse.

Decentralizing power and placing it in confederations of neighbourhoods is desirable on a practical level. This process is advanced through the establishment of assemblies and helped along by co-operative housing and community land trusts. That bureaucrats are wholly ill-equipped to deal with the crises of cities is evidenced plainly by the situation most cities find themselves in. The theory and practice of mutual aid was demystified during the Covid-19 pandemic. That neighbourhood resilience can be established by spontaneous organizing more effectively than the State's delayed response is notable proof of concept.

It is hard not to sense that we may have passed several tipping points: ecologically, politically, and otherwise. However, we find ourselves in a situation defined by inevitables. The radical transformation of our world, our cities, and our ordinary lives is inevitable because capitalism is unsustainable. We cannot continue in this manner and electric cars will not save us. With the imminent and existential threats of climate change and nuclear disaster looming ever-nearer, the pressure is on to build and organize new institutions for power now. If municipalists cannot effectively organize dual power systems now, then States will have no maneuverability left but to morph increasingly into totalitarian technocracies, reacting piecemeal to evermore crises, dominating all aspects of social and private life.

2. Why 'Take the City' as a phrase?

The answer is relatively straightforward. "Take the City" is made in direct reference to Henri Lefebvre's 1968 book, the idea, and eventual slogan, *Le Droit à la ville* (*The Right to the City*). Lefebvre recognized that—under the effects of capitalism (and urbanization)—society had been commodified in a totalizing sense. The idea that citizens have a right to the city, over and above capital interests, became a rallying cry for municipal movements across the world beginning in the late 60s. The title of our book is an attempt to carry forward that idea and to act on it.

Taken by Whom?

The previous two questions generate a third: Taken by whom? The answer, again, is rather straightforward: citizens. But it's worth engaging, who are citizens?

In Montréal, there is an ongoing debate in some organizing circles over the use of the word 'citizen.' Activists have no hesitation using the French *citoyen/citoyenne*, but the English equivalent is deeply embattled, for good reason. Citizen, in much of the anglo-American world, is used with exclusionary intent. In ordinary usage, it tends to suggest a State-sanctioned ability to reside in a particular place and enjoy all of the rights afforded to other full members, as defined by a central state bureaucracy.

It is unfortunate that this term has become so fraught, as the French and English share the same etymological roots. Both relate to the Latin *civitas* or 'city.' Citizenship ought not to be viewed as a Statist category but to denote that all who reside in a city ought to be treated as full, participating, rightful members of the city as a mere result of their residence. But "ought" in the context of ordinary language is fraught.

As the Covid-19 pandemic so clearly displayed, a neighborhood's capacity to meaningfully endure is contingent upon forms of mutual aid which put no stock in technical status, i.e. 'citizenship' as it tends to be used. That the English term has been denigrated to a technical term—one contingent on bureaucracy—is a shame. However, there are few alternatives to 'citizen' for our efforts. Do we fight for the soul of the term? Should we advocate that all residents of a city are by nature citizens, regardless of the State's interpretation, and as such should receive all of the rights and protections of others in their city? I think so, but this section is also intended to spark debate.

It is an absurd situation that a participating member of civil society in society can contribute so much and yet an office potentially hundreds or thousands of miles away can determine the scope of an individual's choices. Immigrants without status face regular, paralyzing choices every day. Whether they should take work, seek out medical advice or treatment, use certain types of transportation, and much else becomes a big decision. A radical municipalist agenda should recognize the absurdity of this situation but consider the implications of the term in their context. In Montréal, for example, the *Montréal Charter of Rights and Responsibilities* ensures citizens "the rights and freedoms proclaimed and guaranteed by the Universal Declaration of Human Rights."[9] The Charter has been employed meaningfully in the city by various community groups to great effect. The Charter relies on the language of 'citizen,' but the term is employed inclusively and liberally, sometimes interchangeably with "Montréaler." The impact of abandoning the term 'citizen' in our organizing in an effort to be more inclusive of those without status can have an inadvertently negative impact. The concept of "local citizenship" in contrast to the nation-state was brought into significant tension during the rise of Sanctuary Cities. Restoring the historic ties between citizenship and municipal residence might have positive implications.

A Brief History of the Montréal Citizens' Movement

The rise and fall of the Montréal Citizens' Movement (MCM) is instructive today for both its successes and failures. Before one can understand the rise of the party, it is important to briefly explain the context in which it was born.

Jean Drapeau was the mayor of Montréal from 1954–57 and 1960–1986. Drapeau's administration was notorious for its corruption, centralization, and authoritarian approach to city politics. His legacy projects included the development of the Montréal Metro system, Expo 67, the performing arts centre, Place des Arts, and the controversial construction of the Olympic stadium. He was the central figure of his municipal party, *Parti Civique* (Civic Party).

In 1960s Québec, Montréal experienced the Quiet Revolution. During this time, the tight grip that the Catholic Church held over the province notably diminished. In the early stages of this era, an alliance was formed between labour and the state and there was significant economic and social development.

By the late 1960s, the relationship between the state and the labour unions was strained. The Confederation of National Trade Unions (CSN) in Québec became increasingly radical, advocating increased union involvement in social issues like housing, unemployment, co-operatives, health insurance, and similar areas. By 1970, a new political party had formed—*Front d'action politique* (FRAP). Led by militant union officials and community organisers, the FRAP adopted a radical municipalist manifesto (translated in the Annex of this book). It was an explicitly socialist project with significant support.

In 1970, the FRAP found itself at the centre of the October Crisis, which culminated in Prime Minister Pierre Trudeau invoking the War Measures Act after Provincial Deputy Premier Pierre Laporte and British diplomat James Cross were kidnapped by members of the *Front de liberation du Québec* (FLQ; Québec Liberation Front), a militant Québec separatist group. Laporte was murdered. Jean Drapeau falsely linked the Crisis to the FRAP, destroying their prospects in the 1970 elections and crippling the Party and leading to its eventual collapse shortly thereafter.

Still, popular discontent with the Drapeau administration and a stalled economy carried on. By 1972, 200,000 workers joined the Québec General Strike and formed a Common Front. The strike ended with a government bill forcing workers back to their jobs. This wave of discontent culminated in the establishment of a new party in 1974, the MCM. The party was founded by a heterogeneous group mostly composed of unions and community groups ahead of the 1974 municipal elections.

The story of the early days of the MCM is captured by the writing of Stephen Schecter, an astute party ideologue who would later become an executive member of the party.[10] He notes that the primary difference between the FRAP and the MCM was that the FRAP had a "working-class orientation" which was "much clearer and consequently, its base much more rooted in the popular groups active in Montréal at the time."[11] The MCM, on the other hand, despite its radical roots had significant theoretical ambiguities from its founding and always had a strong "electoralist mentality."[12]

Despite any ambiguities, the MCM managed to win 18 of 55 seats on the City Council in 1974 with 45.3% of the popular vote.[13] It was a significant and historic victory made possible by grassroots organizing and a diverse coalition of leftists. In its early platform, the MCM included many radical proposals: "the creation of neighbourhood councils with extensive political and economic powers, the gradual implementation of free and expanded public transport, local control of land development, strict enforcement of a revamped housing code,"[14] and many others.

In his informative book, *A City With a Difference: The Rise and Fall of the Montréal Citizens' Movement* (1997), Timothy Lloyd Thomas describes the three general groupings of party members as 1. Ideologues, 2. Pragmatists, and 3. Lobbyists. He explains that what unified the MCM was "the belief that through community control over municipal politics the rigid hierarchy of the existing [Drapeau] administration could be broken."[15] This early period, especially from 1976–1978 was largely influenced by the party ideologues. There was particular tension between Marxist-Leninist elements of the party and libertarian socialists. This struggle is captured in two articles. The first by party-reformist Henry Milner's article on "The Urban Question" and Dimitri Roussopoulos's reply, "Beyond Reformism: The Ambiguity of the Urban Question." Roussopoulos captures the emergent party dynamics when he writes:

> "If one examines the positions on this question of all the current parties on the ideological spectrum from conservative to Marxist-Leninist, they remain the same in essence. One part of the spectrum accepts the political system of electoralism, after all, it was created by the bourgeoisie, while the other claims it wants 'to use the system', as if it is both more clever and more powerful than the system, and as if this is an important way to reach the people."[16]

In response to Milner's emphasis on 'mobilisation' as a political tactic, Roussopoulos writes:

> "Nothing short of the creation of the autonomous self-organisation of the new proletariat will do. Autonomous, so that such a movement cannot be co-opted by either the State or some political party. Self-organisation, so that such a

movement is built from the bottom and relies on its own strength. New Proletariat, so that it is built on class consciousness and advances class-struggle based on a contemporary definition of the exploited and the dominated majority of society. "[17]

In his 1975 article, Roussopoulos notes the party's ambiguous commitment to neighborhood councils. The MCM's lack of clarity on plans regarding councils would later become a fracture point for the party. Roussopoulos was right to express concern; the MCM would later establish District Advisory Committees (DACs) based in the city boroughs, which many activists argued were a "'sham and a facade' because they lacked decision-making powers."[18] The primary tool of the DACs was to submit *requêtes* (requests or queries) which local borough councilors were supposed to debate publicly—a far cry from citizen assemblies with decision-making power. The DACs accomplished very little and would fade in time. Despite the waffling that would come down the line for the MCM, 1975 produced radical internal results. The executive committee submitted a report proposing resolutions for the party to adopt. Roussopoulos notes 2 of the most important:

"1/ "The programme of the MCM stems from a socialist analysis of the city which implies:
a) that the capitalist mode of production is the principal cause of the urban crisis,
b) that consequently our strategy of political action must stem from this socialist analysis of the city,
c) that in the public stances of the party at all levels, we link our immediate demands to this socialist critique of the city.

2/ The first priority to emerge from this analysis is grassaroots mobilization: electoral and parliamentary activity must be situated within this perspective."[19]

While the ideologues defined much of the MCM's activity during the period of 1976–78 and its theoretical position became increasingly interesting, especially in the context of contemporary municipalism, the MCM hit a wall in 1978. With economic uncertainty stewing, even the future of the Canadian state being in question in light of militant separatist movements in Québec, and the departure

Jason Toney

of many centrist pragmatists from the MCM into new parties, Jean Drapeau and his Civic Party dominated the 1978 elections.[20] The MCM was crushed, only winning a single City Council seat. Between 1978–1998, the MCM would have several notable victories, including a two-term mayor in Jean Doré. At one point they would control 55 out of 58 seats in City Council; however, much of that period was dominated by pragmatists and lobbyists, with only a few leftist councillors left who would almost all leave the party on ideological grounds. The 'electoralist mentality' came to dominate most of the party's history and its social victories were minimal, certainly never amounting to the original party goals in the contexts of participatory democracy, housing, and transportation. In fact, by 1998 a former MCM councillor accused the party's executive committee of centralizing power "to almost as great an extent" as had Drapeau's administration, accusing the MCM of being at risk of oligarchy.[21]

Lessons Learned in Montréal

From this all to little-known, remarkable municipalist moment in Montréal's history, we can derive valuable lessons. The MCM was born out of a spontaneous period of radical, grassroots organization in Montréal; however, the movement substituted itself for a political party and became the victim of electoralism, never achieving most of its original goals. Indeed, a conclusion made by Thomas is that many Montréalers, in light of the rise and fall of the MCM, began to recognize that political parties, "even the ones closest to the people, are becoming a less important vehicle for enacting social change originating from the 'grassroots' elements.... It taught Montréalers that local politics does not necessarily depend on municipal administrations, rather on people themselves in their communities."[22] In "The new Urban Left: Parties Without Actors," (1996) an analysis of the MCM and its implications, Eric Shragge and Henri Lustiger-Thaler conclude that the key question for Montréal political actors is how to make space for a "third space" in urban politics and become "fixed agents" rather than merely "situationally political."[23] This question is applicable to all municipal activists, especially in our time, and cuts to the core of the question of how to build dual power and avoid being pigeon-holed into a nexus of non-profits beholden to bureaucratic oversights (namely via State-mandated, coercive requirements to qualify for grant money) which constitute a new industrial complex for services.

These lessons have been passed down to the author. In early 2021, the author was invited to join a group called *Prenons la ville* (Take the City). Some of the core organizers were members of the FRAP and the MCM and helped guide the research herein. *Prenons la ville* is an attempt at forming a coalition of neighbourhood groups ahead of the November 2021 municipal elections. The intent is to collaboratively raise our common struggles and pressure municipal candidates and the eventual administration, without ourselves becoming a political party. *Prenons la ville* is actively working with activists in their neighbourhoods to form citizen assemblies and organize more collaboratively, an activity rarely witnessed in a city of political silos.

A General Overview

This book is a unique collection of the aspirations, successes, and failures of actors from around the world. Indeed, the most important goal for the global municipalist movement today should be to have its ideas articulated in as many ways as possible by as many people as possible. This is a movement led and defined by ordinary people. Before any confederation of municipalities can begin to take form, citizens have to take action in the places they live. In order to be most effective in the effort to democratize our communities, we have to take seriously the task of learning from each other.

Radical municipalism is characterized by its variation. However, the movement today is unified by a rejection of neoliberalism, capitalism, and systems of domination. Policy ought to be crafted at the neighbourhood, municipal, and regional levels by citizen assemblies. These policy decisions can then be administered at appropriate scales by limited, accountable agencies. It is important to note that the top-down policy-making processes that systems of oppression have historically relied on have been evermore embraced by many strands of mainstream progressivism today. This should be met not with just skepticism but outright resistance.

Radical municipalism is a decentralized body of political theory that is not rigid or ideological. There is a sense in which this is a deeply conservative movement. Rejections of top-down style government recall a Tocquevillian view of participatory democracy. The global municipalist movement encourages reading groups and popular education, but it has not relied on deference to the lofty ideals of a handful of long-passed intellectuals. Instead, it has elevated new voices. Organizations like Barcelona en Comú have worked towards the feminization of politics, meaning the fair distribution of political work, action, and labour. The value of this approach cannot be overstated.

The first section on The Challenges Ahead treats municipalism's theoretical backdrop and defines the most pressing issues of our time. Climate chaos, the housing crisis, savage inequalities in wealth, and the grave threats posed by financialization and speculation make this movement ever more urgent.

In the second section on Building Democracy through Municipal Electoral Politics, the respective municipal histories of Red Vienna and Montréal are historicized. The very successful history of Red Vienna has not been widely written about in the English language, and Le Front d'action politique in Montréal even less so. More recent accounts from the cities of Burlington and Barcelona are provided with intimate, narrative details.

In contrast to the second section, the third section on Dual Power and Reclaiming the City Beyond Elections covers the rise of democracy in Bakur, the women's movement in Oaxaca, Cooperation Jackson, and the issues with Montréal's progressive political party, Project Montréal. Taken together, these essays illustrate the tension between organizing within and beyond the existing electoral structures of the State. This tension can easily devolve into antagonism, but many have effectively managed to rethink the dichotomy with admirable results.

The final essays in the concluding section, Possible Futures, envisions societies in transformation. By looking at promising solutions being experimented with today, we are able to glimpse their potential impact and imagine new ways forward. The contributions here treat solidarity cities, the transformative socio-political effect of hip-hop culture, and the path towards a moral economy. Charting a democratic future depends on the act of working together in a manner that is hands-on and face-to-face. This program is sometimes criticized as parochial, but such a dismissive view underestimates the task of building solidarity in a time of unprecedented polarization and loneliness. It is the task of world-making, of building a ship as the floodwaters rise.

Growing masses of people firmly believe we need a new way forward. By taking back our cities, investing in public transportation, re-thinking the commodification of land and labour, protecting our ecosystems, empowering the working classes and oppressed people, constructing moral economies, and establishing participatory democracies based in our neighbourhoods we might resist the gravest existential crises in human history. We might mobilize masses of people around a genuinely democratic program. More than resist, we might transform our cities, our societies, and our planet.

Endnotes

1 Laura Roth, "Municipalist Politics and the Specter of Emancipation,"*Roar*, Issue #10, July 9, 2020, pg. 3.

2 Ibid.

3 The 2018 Revision of World Urbanization Prospects, United Nations Department of Economic and Social Affairs/Population Division, pg. xix.

4 Dimitrios I. Roussopoulos, The Rise of Cities: Montréal, Toronto, Vancouver and Other Cities (Montréal: Black Rose Books, 2017), 7.

5 Murray Bookchin, in Urbanization without Cities: The Rise and Decline of Citizenship (Black Rose Books, 1992), p. 12.

6 Karl Polanyi, The Great Transformation: The Political and Economic Origins of Our Time (Boston: Beacon Press, 2014).

7 Judith Dellheim and Jason Prince, eds., Free Public Transportation: And Why We Don't Pay to Ride Elevators (Black Rose Books, 2018).

8 Transformative planning

9 Montréal Charter of Rights and Responsibilities (Montréal: Ville de Montréal, 2005), 3.

10 Stephen Schecter, The Politics of Urban Liberation (Montréal: Black Rose Books, 1978), 173-176.

11 Schecter, 176.

12 Ibid.

13 Ibid.

14 Schecter 183.

15 Timothy Lloyd Thomas, A City with a Difference: The Rise and Fall of the Montréal CITIZEN'S MOVEMENT (Montréal: Véhicule Press, 1997), 36.

16 Dimitrios Roussopoulos, "Beyond Reformism: The Ambiguity of the Urban Question,"*Our Generation* 11, No. 2, (Winter 1976), 48.

17 Ibid.

Jason Toney

18 Thomas, 132.

19 Roussopoulos, "Beyond Reformism: The Ambiguity of the Urban Question," 54.

20 Thomas, 46.

21 Thomas, 112.

22 Thomas, 140, 150.

23 Henri Lustiger-Thaler and Eric Shragge, "The New Urban Left: Parties without Actors," International Journal of Urban and Regional Research 22, no. 2 (1998): pp. 233-244, https://doi.org/10.1111/1468-2427.00137, 243.

The Challenges Ahead

Communalism Against Climate Chaos

Brian Tokar

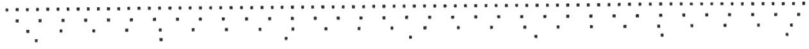

Since the 1960s, the theory and praxis of social ecology have helped guide efforts to articulate a radical, counter-systemic ecological outlook with a goal of transforming society's relationship to non-human nature. For many decades, social ecologists have articulated a fundamental ecological critique of capitalism and the state, and proposed an alternative vision of empowered human communities organized confederally in pursuit of a more harmonious relationship to the wider natural world. Social ecology helped shape the New Left and anti-nuclear movements in the 1960s and 1970s, the emergence of Green politics in many countries, the alter-globalization movement of the late 1990s and early 2000s, and most recently the struggle for democratic autonomy by Kurdish communities in Turkey and Syria, along with the resurgence of new municipal movements around the world.

The philosophical vision of social ecology was first articulated by Murray Bookchin between the early 1960s and the early 2000s, and has since been further elaborated by his colleagues and many others. It is a unique synthesis of social criticism, historical and anthropological investigation, dialectical philosophy and political strategy. Social ecology can be viewed as an unfolding of several distinct layers of understanding and insight, spanning all of these dimensions and more. It begins with an appreciation of the fact that environmental problems are fundamentally *social* and *political* in nature, and are rooted in the historical legacies of domination and social hierarchy.

Capitalism vs. the Climate

Bookchin was among the first thinkers in the West to identify the growth imperative of the capitalist system as a fundamental threat to the integrity of living ecosystems, and he consistently argued that so-

cial and ecological concerns are fundamentally inseparable, question-
ing the narrowly instrumental approaches advanced by many environ-
mentalists to address various issues.

For climate activists today, this encourages an understanding that
a meaningful approach to the climate crisis requires a systemic view
of the centrality of fossil fuel combustion to the emergence and continued resilience of capitalism. Indeed, capitalism as we know it is
virtually inconceivable without the exponential growth in energy usage—and widespread substitutions of energy for labor—that coal, oil
and gas have enabled. As the UK-based Corner House research group
explained in a 2014 paper:

> The entire contemporary system of making profits out of
> labor depended absolutely on cheap fossil carbon [and
> therefore] there is no cheap or politically-feasible substitute
> for fossil fuels in the triple combination of fossil fuels–heat
> engines–commodified labor that underpins current rates of
> capital accumulation.

Fossil fuels have long been central to the capitalist *mythos* of perpetual growth. They have driven ever-increasing concentrations of
capital in many economic sectors, and advanced both the regimenta-
tion and increasing precarity of human labor worldwide. Andreas
Malm explains in detail in *Fossil Capital* how early British industrial-
ists opted to switch from abundant water power to coal-fired steam
engines to run their mills, despite increased costs and uncertain reliab-
ility. The ability to control labor was central to their decision, as the
urban poor proved to be vastly more amenable to factory discipline
than the more independent-minded rural dwellers who lived along
Britain's rapidly flowing rivers. A century later, massive new oil dis-
coveries in the Middle East and elsewhere would drive previously unfathomable increases in the productivity of human labor and breathe
new life into the capitalist myth of unlimited economic expansion.

To address the full magnitude of the climate crisis and maintain a
habitable planet for future generations we need to shatter that myth
once and for all. Today the political supremacy of fossil fuel interests
far transcends the magnitude of their campaign contributions or their
short-term profits. It stems from their continuing central role in advancing the very system they helped to create. We need to overturn

both fossil fuels and the growth economy, and that will require a fundamental rethinking of many of the core underlying assumptions of contemporary societies.

The Philosophy of Social Ecology

Fortunately for this, social ecology has evolved well beyond the level of critique. In the 1970s, Bookchin engaged in extensive research into the evolution of the relationship between human societies and non-human nature. His writing challenged the common Western notion that humans inherently seek to dominate the natural world, concluding instead that the domination of nature is a myth rooted in relationships of domination among people that emerged from the breakdown of ancient tribal societies in Europe and the Middle East.

Social ecology highlights egalitarian social principles that many indigenous cultures—both past and present—have held in common, and has elevated these as guideposts for a renewed social order: concepts such as interdependence, reciprocity, unity-in-diversity and an ethics of complementarity, that is, the balancing of roles among various social sectors by actively compensating for differences among individuals. In his magnum opus, *The Ecology of Freedom*, Bookchin detailed the unfolding conflicts between these guiding principles and those of increasingly stratified hierarchical societies, and how this has shaped the contending legacies of domination and freedom for much of human history.

Beyond this, the philosophical inquiry of social ecology examines the emergence of human consciousness from within the processes of natural evolution. Reaching back to the roots of dialectical thought, from Aristotle to Hegel, Bookchin advanced a unique approach to eco-philosophy, emphasizing the potentialities that lie latent within the evolution of both natural and social phenomena while celebrating the uniqueness of human creativity and self-reflection. Social ecology eschews the common view of nature as merely a realm of necessity, instead perceiving nature as striving, in a sense, to actualize through evolution an underlying potentiality for consciousness, creativity and freedom.

For Bookchin, a dialectical outlook on human history compels us to reject what merely is and follow the potentialities inherent in evolution toward an expanded view of what could be, and ultimately what ought to be. While the realization of a free, ecological society is far from inevitable—and may appear ever less likely in the face of impending climate chaos—it is perhaps the most rational outcome of four billion years of natural evolution.

Political Strategy

These historical and philosophical explorations in turn provide an underpinning for social ecology's revolutionary political strategy, which has been discussed previously in *ROAR Magazine* by several social ecology colleagues. This strategy is generally described as libertarian or confederal municipalism, or more simply as *communalism*, stemming from the legacy of the Paris Commune of 1871.

Like the communards, Bookchin argued for liberated cities, towns and neighborhoods governed by open popular assemblies. He believed that the confederation of such liberated municipalities could overcome the limits of local action, allowing cities, towns and neighborhoods to sustain a democratic counter-power to the centralized political institutions of the state, all while overcoming parochialism, promoting interdependence and advancing a broad liberatory agenda. Furthermore, he argued that the stifling anonymity of the capitalist market can be replaced by a moral economy in which economic as well as political relationships are guided by an ethics of mutualism and reciprocity.

Social ecologists believe that whereas institutions of capitalism and the state heighten social stratification and exploit divisions among people, alternative structures rooted in direct democracy can foster the expression of a general social interest towards social and ecological renewal. "It is in the municipality," Bookchin wrote in *Urbanization Without Cities*, "that people can reconstitute themselves from isolated monads into a creative body politic and create an existentially vital ... civic life that has institutional form as well as civic content."

People inspired by this view have brought structures of direct democracy through popular assemblies into numerous social movements in the US, Europe and beyond, from popular direct-action campaigns against nuclear power in the late 1970s to the more recent alter-globalization and Occupy Wall Street movements. The prefigurative dimension of these movements—anticipating and enacting the various elements of a liberated society—has encouraged participants to challenge the status quo while advancing transformative visions of the future. The concluding chapter of my recent book, *Toward Climate Justice* (New Compass 2014) describes these influences in some detail, with a focus on the anti-nuclear movement, green politics, eco-feminism and other significant currents from the past and present.

Contributions to Contemporary Movements

Today, social ecologists are actively engaged in the global movement for climate justice, which unites converging currents from a variety of sources, most notably indigenous and other land-based people's movements from the Global South, environmental justice campaigners from communities of color in the Global North, and continuing currents from the global justice or alter-globalization movements of a decade ago. It is worth considering some of social ecology's distinct contributions to this broad-based climate justice movement in some greater detail.

First, social ecology offers an uncompromising ecological outlook that challenges the entrenched power structures of capitalism and the nation-state. A movement that fails to confront the underlying causes of environmental destruction and climate disruption can, at best, only superficially address those problems. Climate justice activists generally understand, for example, that false climate solutions such as carbon markets, geoengineering and the promotion of natural gas obtained from fracking as a "bridge fuel" on the path to renewable energy mainly serve the system's imperative to keep growing. To fully address the causes of climate change requires movement actors to raise long-range, transformative demands that the dominant economic and political systems may prove unable to accommodate.

Second, social ecology offers a lens to better comprehend the origins and historical emergence of ecological radicalism, from the nascent movements of the late 1950s and early 1960s right up to the present. Social ecology played a central role in challenging the inherent anti-ecological bias of much of twentieth-century Marxism-Leninism, and thus serves as an important complement to current efforts to reclaim Marx's ecological legacy. While the understanding of Marx's long-ignored ecological writings, advanced by authors such as John Bellamy Foster and Kohei Saito, is central to the emerging eco-left tradition, so are the political debates and theoretical insights that unfolded over many pivotal decades when the Marxist left was often vehemently uninterested in environmental matters.

Third, social ecology offers the most comprehensive treatment of the origins of human social domination and its historical relationship to abuses of the Earth's living ecosystems. Social ecology highlights the origins of ecological destruction in social relations of domination, in contrast to conventional views suggesting that impulses to dominate non-human nature are a product of historical necessity. To meaningfully address the climate crisis will require overturning numerous manifestations of the long historical legacy of domination, and an intersectional movement aimed toward challenging social hierarchy in general.

Fourth, social ecology offers a comprehensive historical and strategic grounding for realizing the promise of direct democracy. Social ecologists have worked to bring the praxis of direct democracy into popular movements since the 1970s, and Bookchin's writings offer an essential historical and theoretical context for this continuing conversation. Social ecology offers a comprehensive strategic outlook that looks beyond the role of popular assemblies as a form of public expression and outrage, looking toward more fully realized self-organization, confederation and a revolutionary challenge to entrenched statist institutions.

Finally, social ecology asserts the inseparability of effective oppositional political activity from a reconstructive vision of an ecological future. Bookchin viewed most popular dissident writing as incomplete, focusing on critique and analysis without also proposing a coherent way forward. At the same time, social ecologists have spoken out against the accommodation of many alternative institutions—including numerous formerly radical cooperatives and collectives—to a stifling capitalist status quo.

The convergence of oppositional and reconstructive strands of activity is a crucial step towards a political movement that can ultimately contest and reclaim political power. This is realized within the international climate movement through the creation of new political spaces that embody the principles of "blockadia" and "alternatiba." The former term, popularized by Naomi Klein, was first coined by the activists of the Tar Sands Blockade in Texas, who engaged in an extended series of nonviolent actions to block the construction of the Keystone XL oil pipeline. The latter is a French Basque word, adopted as the theme of a bicycle tour that encircled France during the summer of 2015 and highlighted scores of local alternative-building projects. Social ecology's advocacy for creative human participation in the natural world helps us see how we can radically transform our communities, while healing and restoring vital ecosystems through a variety of sophisticated, ecologically-grounded methods.

Global Inertia, Municipal Responses

Following the celebrated but ultimately disappointing conclusion of the 2015 UN climate conference in Paris, many climate activists have embraced a return to the local. While the Paris Agreement is widely praised by global elites—and activists rightly condemned the US Trump administration's announced withdrawal—the agreement has a fundamental flaw that largely precludes the possibility of its achieving meaningful climate mitigation.

This flaw emerged from Barack Obama and Hillary Clinton's interventions at the 2009 Copenhagen climate conference, which shifted the focus of climate diplomacy from the 1997 Kyoto Protocol's legally binding emissions reductions toward a system of voluntary pledges, or "Nationally Determined Contributions," which now form the basis of the Paris framework. Implementation and enforcement of the agreement are limited to what the Paris text describes as an international "expert-based" committee that is structured to be "transparent, non-adversarial and non-punitive." Of course the Kyoto regime also lacked meaningful enforcement mechanisms and countries such as Canada and Australia chronically exceeded their Kyoto-mandated emissions caps. The Kyoto Protocol initiated an array of "flexible mechanisms" to implement emissions reductions, leading to the global proliferation of carbon markets, dubious offset schemes, and other capitalist-inspired measures that have largely benefited financial interests without meaningful benefits to the climate. While the original 1992 UN Climate Convention enshrined various principles aimed to address the inequalities among nations, subsequent climate diplomacy has often resembled a demoralizing race to the bottom.

In response to the announced US withdrawal from the Paris climate agreement, an alliance of over 200 US cities and counties announced their intention to uphold the cautious but still significant commitments that the Obama administration had brought to Paris. Internationally, more than 2,500 cities from Oslo to Sydney have submitted plans to the United Nations to reduce their greenhouse gas emissions, sometimes in defiance of their national governments' far more cautious commitments.

Two local popular *consultas* in Columbia moved to reject mineral and oil exploitation within their territories, in one case affiliating their town with the Italian-based "Slow Cities" movement—an outgrowth of the famous Slow Food movement that has helped raise the social and cultural standing of local food producers in Italy and many other countries. A Slow Cities statement of principles suggests that by "working towards sustainability, defending the environment and reducing our excessive ecological footprint," communities are "committing ... to rediscover traditional know-how and to make the most of our resources through recycling and reuse, applying the new technologies."

The ability of such municipal movements to build support and pressure for broader institutional changes is central to their political importance in a period when social and environmental progress is stalled in many countries. Actions initiated from below may also have more staying power than those mandated from above. They are far more likely to be democratically structured and accountable to people who are most affected by the outcomes. They help build relationships among neighbors and strengthen the capacity for self-reliance. They enable us to see that the institutions that now dominate our lives are far less essential for our daily sustenance than we are often led to believe. And, perhaps most important, such municipal initiatives can challenge regressive measures implemented from above, as well as national policies that favor fossil fuel corporations and allied financial interests.

For the most part, recent municipal initiatives in the US and beyond have evolved in a progressive direction. Over 160 US cities and counties have declared themselves as "sanctuaries" in defiance of the Trump administration's elevated enforcement of US immigration laws—a very important development in light of the future displacements that will result from climate change. Such ongoing political and legal battles over the rights of municipalities against states speak to the radical potential of socially and ecologically progressive measures emerging from below.

Social and environmental justice activists in the US are also challenging the trend of right-wing electoral victories by running and winning bold campaigns for a variety of municipal positions. Perhaps most noteworthy is the successful 2017 campaign of Chokwe Antar Lumumba, who was elected mayor of Jackson, Mississippi, in the heart of the Deep South, with a program focused on human rights, local democracy and neighborhood-based economic and ecological renewal. Lumumba ran as the voice of a movement known as Co-operation Jackson, which takes its inspiration from the Black American tradition and the Global South, including the resistance struggles of enslaved Africans before and after the US Civil War, the Zapatista movement in southern Mexico, and recent popular uprisings around the globe.

Cooperation Jackson has put forward numerous ideas that resonate strongly with the principles of social ecology, including empowered neighborhood assemblies, cooperative economics and a dual-power political strategy. Others working to resist the status quo and build local power are organizing directly democratic neighborhood assemblies from New York City to the Pacific Northwest, and developing a new national network to further advance municipalist strategies, as Eleanor Finley importantly recounted in her essay on "The New Municipal Movements" in *ROAR* #6.

Visions of the Future

Whether local efforts such as these can help usher in a coherent and unified municipalist movement in solidarity with "rebel city" initiatives around the world still remains to be seen. Such a movement will be necessary for local initiatives to ultimately catalyze the world-scale transformations that are necessary to fend off the looming threat of a complete breakdown in the Earth's climate systems.

Indeed, the projections of climate science continually highlight the difficulty of transforming our societies and economies quickly enough to prevent a descent into a planet-wide climate catastrophe. But science also affirms that the actions we undertake today can mean the difference between a future climate regime that is disruptive and difficult, and one that rapidly descends toward apocalyptic extremes. While we need to be completely realistic about the potentially devastating consequences of continuing climate disruptions, a genuinely transformative movement needs to be rooted in a forward-looking view of an improved quality of life for most people in the world in a future freed from fossil fuel dependence.

Partial measures are far from sufficient, and approaches to renewable energy development that merely replicate capitalist forms may likely turn out to be a dead end. However, the cumulative impact of municipal efforts to challenge entrenched interests and actualize living alternatives—combined with coherent revolutionary visions, organization and strategies toward a radically transformed society—could perhaps be enough to fend off a dystopian future of deprivation and authoritarianism.

Democratically confederated municipalist initiatives remain our best hope to meaningfully reshape the future. Perhaps the threat of climate chaos, combined with our deep knowledge of the potential for a more humane and ecologically harmonious future, can indeed help inspire the profound transformations that are necessary for humanity and the Earth to continue to thrive.

"Communalism Against Climate Chaos" was originally published by Roar Magazine. Issue #7 (Autumn 2017): 28-39.

The Crisis of Late Capitalism in Seattle

Robert Kaminski

The early 1800s were terrible times to be a British peasant. Parliament had been steadily granting landlords' requests for enclosure since the 1500s, fencing off common land used by peasants for communal subsistence gardening. The landlords got a great deal; the newly vacant land could be used to produce more commodifiable goods (usually wool, but also minerals). The peasants were not as lucky. Stripped of their homes, communities, and food, the dispossessed were forced to sell themselves for subsistence. Many showed up starving and desperate for wages on the streets of the booming industrial and port towns.

British cities at the time were not healthy places. Laborers as young as five, working nearly 3,600 hours per year by 1840 (compared with 1,440 in the 1300s), faced severe injury or death working 16-hour days in the factories. The average life expectancy in towns like Manchester was 20 to 30 years lower than the countryside.[1]

Faced with sudden explosions in homelessness and debt, Parliament responded with a militarized criminalization of poverty. Countless people were swept off the streets and impressed into the British Navy. Others were shipped around the world to the American and Australian penal colonies,[2] themselves nearly purged of their large indigenous populations by British and European imperialists.

The working class had little political recourse. Standing or voting for Parliament was restricted to landowning men—the very people responsible for so much working-class misery. Around 98% of the population was completely excluded from the political process. The world was being radically reshaped by the world's richest with no concern for those at the margins.

Fast forward to Seattle in 2018 and we have analogous problems: an exploding homeless population that regularly endures forced eviction, powerful corporate developers vacuuming up city blocks and public land, entire communities being displaced, a global environmental crisis, and governments that remain unresponsive to the most marginalized communities' needs.

If we are to address these problems in a meaningful way, we must first recognize that these problems are neither unique nor isolated. Rather, the conjunction of massive racial and economic inequality, global climate breakdown, and widespread housing crises are all parts of the structural crisis of globalized neoliberal capitalism. The system isn't failing; it's operating exactly as designed.

Supply or Demand?

Take housing. In King County, the unhoused and housing-insecure population is over 10,000 strong. According to market logic, this must signify an absolute housing shortage. In fact, the opposite is the case—as of December 2016, there were over 200,000 empty bedrooms in King County.[3] Most of these are in single-family homes in outlying areas far from job markets[4] and without good transit (by design), but many are not—Capitol Hill's echo-y mansions could easily fit more people. Amid this flush supply of empty bedrooms, prices for even leaky century-old houses with lead pipes are skyrocketing.[5]

Of course, this argument is not complete. The market-based argument counters with some variation of "people want to live in vibrant places," which is true but generally contradicts market theory. The physical demand for housing is most acute for the 51% of Seattle tax filers who earn under $50,000 per year,[6] yet the only housing being built is structurally unaffordable. Existing housing prices are kept massively inflated by speculation. And the strongest defense of the current system is, essentially, "rich people have high demand for culture."

That culture is usually created by people who need cheap housing—people of color, queer communities, artists, writers, students, etc. Gentrification can be interpreted as commodification and extraction of that culture, to be accumulated by landowners in the form of exorbitant rent. Often this process includes displacement of those low-income, cultural communities, leaving only token allusions to the former residents like rainbow sidewalks or indigenous place names. Under contemporary late capitalism, living in "the gay neighborhood" or "historic neighborhoods" is another wealth signifier magically worth an extra $500 in rent or $50,000 in house value, not unlike the garish and confusing features of your average McMansion.[7] And that doesn't even touch the rooftop barbecues.

Housing is a Structural Crisis of Market Capitalism and Landlords Like It That Way

Inflated housing value would be bad enough if it were isolated to small, individually- or family-owned structures like detached houses. Land consolidation by corporate developers is much more pressing. Take Roosevelt Station, scheduled to open in 2021. Seattle has been allowing large companies to purchase entire blocks near the station—often a dozen individual lots or more—to construct single buildings on the newly huge plats. Most of the housing in the station's walkshed—a few thousand units, at least—is owned by a small handful of investment firms.

This pattern is nightmarish, and not just because tower- and block-scale construction may not even lead to appreciable walkability or density.[8] Instead, it is a large-scale concentration of power and land ownership in a time of skyrocketing inequality.

Just like the Industrial Revolution-era British landlords, Seattle real estate investors are primarily interested in making lots of money. Renters' and landlords' interests are diametrically opposed—renters want cheap rent with the opportunity of ownership (i.e., a path to not paying rent at all); landlords want permanent rent-paying tenants who will pay ever-growing rents. In this sense, housing is an extractive industry like fossil fuels or old growth logging—only the resource being extracted is our financial livelihood.

Housing is also a growing battleground in modern class conflict. Seattle is quickly becoming a town of perpetually impoverished renters subjugated to a rentier class that owns a growing share of the city's land and housing. Meanwhile, housing insecurity is feeding the ballooning unhoused population that faces arbitrary forced eviction by the police state[9] and slashed social services.[10]

At the base of the housing debates in Seattle, we must recognize that this land was all violently stolen from indigenous people by

an earlier generation of extractors. Today Seattle has a large population of indigenous people who are disproportionately unhoused. In
other words, the ancestral stewards of this land are more likely to be
kicked around by "private owners" whose only attachment to the
land is value extraction.

Talking Solutions

Any sustainable urban policy—housing, transportation, food
production—is doomed to fail without a robust human rights agenda.
This cannot be done without challenging the market system and the
commodification of essential human rights—both inside and outside
formal political institutions.

The biggest obstacle to solving this crisis is breaking through the
narrow logic of market capitalism. Under this regime, housing and land
are commodities to be traded on the global speculative market. As is the
case in Seattle, this often has little bearing in the real economy. Housing
is seen as a financial investment to maximize profit, extracted in the
form of rent, from as many housing units on as much land as possible.
This type of logic is blind to issues of land use, pollution, and human or
environmental suffering. Forgoing the twisted profit imperative—and
challenging the concept of ownership itself, to the point of "rebuilding
the commons"—opens up a wider set of options.

Two promising structurally affordable housing models are gain-
ing in popularity: limited equity housing cooperatives and community
land trusts.[11] Both models are based in collectively owning and/or
managing housing and land. In the cooperative model members own
all property collectively and individually have the right to occupy their
unit (typically in a building). Community land trusts own land in
common and own their individual unit (typically a house) separately.
In both models, the sale prices of units are controlled in some way to
ensure continued affordability over time.

The unifying features of these models are collective ownership,
stewardship, and direct democracy. In effect, this allows for residents
to share housing costs and takes housing off the speculative market.
More importantly they offer affordable long-term housing options, a
supportive community, and meaningful decision-making power. To
challenge the power of extractive landlords, we must build collective
power to take control of our own land and housing.

These cooperative, community-owned institutions are already in place throughout the region, and the work they are doing is far beyond the scope of investment firms. A favorite Seattle-based example is the Lopez Community Land Trust on Lopez Island. They have constructed six housing projects on Lopez Island. Most are net-zero energy and include permaculture gardens, all at relatively low cost. How many Vulcan buildings are net-negative energy permaculture structures?

Challenges and Potential

Barriers to widespread cooperative housing remain, the largest is financial. Despite the growing number of Seattle rental cooperatives (where the house/structure is owned by a landlord), piecing together enough money for buyouts is difficult.

Most community land trusts rely on long fundraising campaigns and financial partnerships with other organizations, much like the Africatown/Forterra project[12] announced last year. Individual organizations get creative. The Lopez CLT often draws skilled community members to volunteer labor, for example. Some generous folks have even donated houses to land trusts for almost nothing. Local credit unions, such as Verity, have begun discussing loan options to cooperative and community-owned projects. Still, the financial difficulties are pressing.

The work of building resilient social infrastructure is nearly as tough. Functioning cooperatives are built on social cohesion and trust—two things that get short shrift in America. Building small 'D' democratic structures and sharing arrangements can be tricky, as anyone who has ever had an argument over dishwashing knows. Luckily, there are plenty of cooperative veterans and resources centers eager to share knowledge, like the Northwest Cooperative Development Center.

The work is rewarding, though, particularly for those traditionally disempowered by the racist global market economy that exploits indigenous people and communities of color.[13] Cooperative ownership can allow folks to build wealth—in the economic and social sense—while reconnecting to each other and the land. It's not inconceivable for such community-owned projects to be key parts of reparations for Indigenous and African-American groups. Indeed, these cooperative economies are thriving in places as disparate as Chiapas, Mexico[14] and Emilia-Romagna, Italy.[15]

Taking the Right to the City around the World

Of course, none of these patterns are new. Displacement and the rebuilding of the city have been used as tools by the powerful for centuries, much like the 1800s British landlords. The popular phrase "the Right to the City" captures the fierce resistance to gentrification; first coined by sociologist Henri Lefebvre in 1968, it has been put by anthropologist David Harvey as "far more than the individual liberty to access urban resources: it is a right to change ourselves by changing the city."[16] It is a fundamental challenge to the status quo political economy of a city by and for technocrats and the global ultra-rich; it is a cry for collective self-determination by the most disenfranchised being taken up around the world.

Barcelona faces many similar problems as Seattle. Barcelonans endure crushing rents and endless waves of exploitative tourism—another form of gentrification. The radical grassroots movement Barcelona en Comu swept into the city government in 2015, less than a year after its founding, capturing 25% of the city council[17] and putting housing organizer Ada Colau in the Mayor's office.[18] The party's core is radical participatory democracy and rebuilding the public sphere after decades of privatization, including expanding public housing and the region's thriving network of cooperatives.

Cooperation Jackson has similarly reshaped Jackson, Mississippi. The organization is a wide network of housing, food, and worker cooperatives built on social and environmental justice principles—a tall order in the Deep South. A prominent organizer with the organization—Chokwe Antar Lumumba—was overwhelmingly elected to the mayor's office last year.

At home in Seattle we have seen an explosion of groups fighting for these same principles. The prominent Housing for All Coalition has secured a string of political victories since kicking off last year. And at the City's latest hearing on the Fort Lawton redevelopment, hundreds representing organizations from the Seattle Democratic Socialists of America to tech solidarity organizations came out to push for affordable housing.[19] Our own Right to the City Movement is taking off in front of our eyes.

The main lesson from these movements is that rights to housing, to the city, to a healthy community and environment are won through major grassroots mobilizations and deliberately building resilient social infrastructures. When we realize our collective power, we can change the world for ourselves and our communities. Given the scale of suffering caused by this structural crisis of capitalism, we must build and wield that power—because billions of lives depend upon it.

Endnotes

1 Martin Daunton, "London's 'Great Stink' and Victorian Urban Planning," BBC, published November 4, 2004, http://www.bbc.co.uk/history/trail/victorian_britain/social_conditions/victorian_urban_planning_01.shtml.

2 Suemedha Sood, "Australia's Penal Colony Roots," BBC, published January 26, 2012, http://www.bbc.com/travel/story/20120126-travelwise-australias-penal-colony-roots.

3 Tom Trimbath, "King County Has at Least 200,000 Empty Beds," Curbed Seattle, published December 19, 2016, https://seattle.curbed.com/2016/12/19/13990918/king-county-empty-bedrooms-housing-supply-seattle-affordability.

4 Dan Bertolet, "Some Neighborhoods Losing Population, Despite the Boom," Sightline Institute, published May 4, 2017, https://www.sightline.org/2017/05/04/some-neighborhoods-losing-population-despite-the-boom/.

5 Sarah Anne Lloyd, "40% of Seattle Homes are Listed at $1M or More," Curbed Seattle, published March 15, 2017, https://seattle.curbed.com/2017/3/15/14930886/seattle-homes-listed-million-dollars.

6 Charles Mudede, "Seattle is a City with Hella Broke People," The Stranger, published August 31, 2017, https://www.thestranger.com/slog/2017/08/31/25388370/seattle-is-a-city-with-a-hell-of-lot-of-broke-people/comments/6.

7 Katie Wagner, "McMansion, USA," Jacobin, published November 9, 2017, https://jacobinmag.com/2017/11/mcmansions-housing-architecture-rich-people.

8 Andrew Price, "Surprising Approaches to Achieving Density," Strong Towns, published January 3, 2018, https://www.strongtowns.org/journal/2018/1/3/comparing-approaches-to-achieving-density.

9 Dae Shik Kim Hawkins Jr, "Political Pulpit: What Progressives Do with Their Homeless," South Seattle Emerald, published December 24, 2017, https://southseattleemerald.com/2017/12/24/column-political-pulpit-what-progressives-do-with-their-homeless/.

10 Melissa Hellman, "Homeless Service Providers Refute City's Reason for Budget Cuts," Seattle Weekly, published December 18, 2017, https://www.seattleweekly.com/news/homeless-service-providers-refute-citys-reason-for-budget-cuts/.

11 Doug Trumm, "The Role of Community Land Trusts in Social Housing," The Urbanist, published June 29, 2016, https://www.theurbanist.org/2016/06/29/the-role-of-community-land-trusts-in-affordability-housing/.

12 "Africatown, Forterra Part of Partnership to Redevelop Midtown Center," The C is for Crank, published May 23, 2017, https://thecisfor-crank.com/2017/05/23/africatown-forterra-part-of-partnership-to-redevelop-midtown-center/.

13 Rakesh Kochhar and Richard Fry, "Wealth Inequality has Widened Along Racial, Ethnic Lines Since End of Great Recession," Pew Research Center, published December 12, 2014, https://www.pewresearch.org/fact-tank/2014/12/12/racial-wealth-gaps-great-recession/.

14 Bill Wilen, "Chiapas Trips Continue to Inspire," The Center for Global Justice, published June 2017, https://www.globaljusticecenter.org/content/chiapas-trips-continue-inspire.

15 John Duda, "The Italian Region Where Co-ops Produce a Third of it's GDP," Yes!, published July 5th, 2016, https://www.yesmagazine.org/new-economy/the-italian-place-where-co-ops-drive-the-economy-and-most-people-are-members-20160705.

16 David Harvey, "The Right to the City," New Left Review, published September 2008, https://newleftreview.org/issues/II53/articles/david-harvey-the-right-to-the-city.

17 ROAR Collective, "Grassroots Movements Sweep into Barcelona Town Hall," ROAR, published May 25, 2015, https://roarmag.org/essays/barcelona-comu-election-victory/.

18 Dan Hancox, "Is This the World's Most Radical Mayor?," The Guardian, published May 26, 2016, https://www.theguardian.com/world/2016/may/26/ada-colau-barcelona-most-radical-mayor-in-the-world.

19 Heidi Groover, "We Went to Magnolia Expecting NIMBYs and Found a Bunch of Housing Supporters Instead," The Stranger, published January 10, 2018, https://www.thestranger.com/slog/2018/01/10/25696995/we-went-to-magnolia-expecting-nimbys-and-found-a-bunch-of-housing-supporters-instead.

Three Lectures on Radical Urbanism

Peter Marcuse, Margit Mayer, and David Harvey

Editors note: The following lectures were all delivered at the City University of New York Graduate Center for the Radical Urbanism Conference on December 12, 2008. Each was edited for readability.

Peter Marcuse

I want to comment on two things having to do with the title of this conference. One is what "Radical Urbanism" is and the other is what the "Right to the City Alliance" is.

I don't want to try to convince you, in the time I have, that it is the right analysis of what is going on in the world. Although, I think it is. I do want to convince you that it is a coherent explanation of what is going on in the world, particularly in the urban area, in which much of what goes on in the world is congealed. And I want to be a little more specific and suggest that while it has a great deal in common with liberal, communitarian, and other critical approaches to the analysis of urban issues, it has also some clear distinctions and those distinctions seem to me to be important, and I would list five as of particular significance.

The first is that it connects issues and developments together and sees them as interrelated. I was at a discussion at Columbia University a couple of weeks ago where Steven Greenhouse spoke, he is the labor reporter for the New York Times. He's written a very good book called *The Big Squeeze: Tough Time for American Workers*, which is full of both data and anecdotes about the difficulties that have been caused to working people in the US these days. But it struck me as on the liberal side of the liberal-radical line. He started out by saying that in the six years after November 2001, we see a big disconnect. Corporate profits nearly doubled, productivity per worker rose 18% while wages remained flat. He went on to argue that this was immoral and described how bad it was. But disconnect? It seems to me that the radical formulation is that we have seen, in the last ten years, that corporate profits have doubled because of worker productivity. That relationship of exploitation, between those who profit on the corporate level and those who suffer at the working level, is central to a radical explanation of what is happening.

The second characteristic that I want to emphasize is that the system can be named, and the name of the system is not a free market system, nor is it a democratic system, although it speaks to a different dimension of it. The name of the system is capitalism. It is a term that has fallen out of fashion by and large in our discussions. But it seems to me that when the Washington Post can put on its front page a headline reading, "Is American Capitalism Dead?," then we can also take it as part of legitimate discourse. The boundary of legitimate discourse is flexible and getting broader. And when someone like Samuel P. Huntington can say that it is the Mexican presence in the US that is subversive and that it is a threat to the United States, that is broadening the limits of the logically permissible pretty widely. But it is not stretching those limits to speak of capitalism and, I think to the extent that it is a correct analysis, it ought to be said more often.

Thirdly, the question of the alternatives, this is a big one. We tend to speak of alternatives in terms of the immediately feasible, and thus the mild alternative is 'a little more regulation' and the big alternatives are 'a lot more regulation,' but regulation of the same thing. And the suggestion that there is an alternative, that it isn't the regulation of the thing, but the thing itself that needs to be changed—I think is a radical approach.

The fourth issue that distinguishes radical approaches is a view of democracy and decision making that does not aim, at least in the foreseeable future, at a consensus. I say this in particular for those of us that deal in urban planning, and the kind of program I teach in, where there is a real strain that defines planning as achieving consensus around specific issues of development. I think that is dead wrong and inconsistent with the way the world works, at least as radical approaches see it. Changes are not all win-win changes—and ought not to be seen that way—they ought to be seen as changes in which what helps some is likely to hurt others. What is at issue is a change in power relations. Those are not win-win changes, those are win-lose changes. And the purpose is that some will lose and others will win.

And the final point is connected with an early paper I wrote called "The Myth of the Benevolent State." It critiqued the idea that the history of policy, both on urban issues and generally, was a history of a benevolent state gradually learning over time how better to achieve benevolent goals, and in each year we learn from our past mistakes and get better and better at what we do. The implication is that the way to influence decisions is through rational persuasion. There is nothing wrong with rational persuasion, I think it needs to be used, but I think it would be a fallacy and a delusion to think that it is rational persuasion that will change relations of power. I think we need all the arguments we can muster. We need also all the organization we can muster, all the power that we have both economically and politically. Persuasion will help with some, but it will not be all, at least if addressed to the state. That which will convince and shape the policies of the incoming administration will not be eloquence or articulateness of the way in which we present what we think ought to be done, it will lie in the mobilization behind those programs.

So that is the way, at least, I see Radical Urbanism. It seems to me a coherent, logical, viable explanation. If there are others, you should explore them. If you find one better—fine—please let me and others know.

The second question I want to address has to do with the Right to the City Alliance. The 'alliance' word is one that is based on a national group in the United States, which brings together groups both geographically, spatially, and sectorally by area of deprivation and area of issue. It brings together homeless groups, gay and lesbian groups, immigrant groups, and students into an alliance. And the question is, is this alliance, or is this conceptualization, a formulation of who the agent of change would be? Of who the actors are, what the entities are, that can in fact implement what we propose—I've spoken of "expose, propose, politicize," when we politicize who is going to be the political force. And I think that needs careful analysis. It is not simply a question of who happens to come to a rally we call around some issue in which we are all agreed—help for those suffering in New Orleans after Katrina—we call a meeting, it is called by the Right to the City Alliance, and that is its constituency. We've got to go beyond that, I think it takes an analysis of who, both objectively and subjectively, is likely to be on the side of wishing to implement a radical urban program.

I think there are two ways of looking at the definition of those with an interest in fundamental change. One is to include the materially deprived. Generally, along class lines, we're used to looking at income inequality, but we're not quite as used to looking at class relations or using the word exploitation. It has to do with material goods, their distribution, the manner of their distribution, and to some extent the manner of their production as well. It certainly has its source in their manner of production. That's one basis, and to the extent that people understand that some people are poor because they are exploited by others who are rich, or are in a different relationship to the forces of production. I think that's a solid basis for understanding for who is likely to be among those supporting fundamental change. What is needed is a recognition that the source of their exploitation, the source of inequality, is a common one and it is called capitalism.

The others that are likely to be involved in movements for fundamental change are people like most of those in this room, who are not appropriately, relatively, called materially deprived, but who might—if they indulged in self-reflection—consider themselves as culturally oppressed. Limited in the freedom to choose what they want to do with their lives. Limited in the way they can express their creativity. Limited in the ways in which they are treated by others that ought to see them equals and colleagues but see them in narrow, defined, and rigidly constrained relationships. And it seems to me a critical task—and one that I hope this conference will help us to face up to—is bringing together those who are materially deprived and those who are culturally oppressed. I include under culturally oppressed certainly those that feel we live in a world with mammoth injustices that need to be remedied and that are uncomfortable if they don't act towards a remedy of those injustices. I think what's needed is to bring those groups together into the kind of movements, the beginnings of which we saw in 1968 in Paris, in Berlin, in New York, and at Columbia. I think one needs, in bringing those groups together, to give priority to the immediate needs of those that are materially deprived.

That is, I don't think that the demand for student participation in departmental government should have precedence over the demand for housing for the homeless. But I think that the two demands do need to come together, ultimately, if fundamental change is to be achieved. And I think we can expect to be successful in that effort, ultimately.

The formulation was already quoted here earlier today, "we are many and they are few." We *are* many and they *are* few. If all of those that are here continue with a commitment to deal with the injustices and inequities that we see about us, that are increasing as we have heard, and that can be remedied because there are alternatives that analysis would suggest, then I think that we will have really accomplished something. I would hope that the formulation "expose, propose, politicize" that I suggested earlier might be one formulation of how to do that. The students have put little stickers in many of the programs that say "expose, propose, politicize." That might be a good thing to have on your refrigerator, but it is certainly a good thing to do. If we can contribute to that process by conferences such as this, we will have accomplished a good bit.

Margit Mayer

The three features that seem the most important to me about the contemporary situation go as follows: 1. The states' response so far to the Great Recession; 2. How the Great Recession is perceived by Capital, who at this point seems to be the major actor in defining and reacting to the Great Recession; 3. Urban conflict and local social movements.

The state is obviously a huge part of the equation, and its reactions have been looked at from various perspectives, but some of them haven't been sufficiently highlighted. Not only has the state, in the course of the last three decades, shrank materially. It has also been re-orienting from welfare to workfare, with a strong bend towards corporate welfare, and has expanded its repressive apparatus. Surveillance capacities, police forces and all kinds of special forces have been growing in various countries, liberal as well as so-called social-democratic European countries. We have seen the growth of zero tolerance and the development of new surveillance technologies, as well as new "soft" weapons such as tasers. These new kinds of instruments have been employed in Germany, where academics who were simply doing research on gentrification were jailed under the new terrorism law. These are no mere accidents: the reduction of civil liberties, the restriction of political freedoms and of the right to demonstrate are all part of a strategy to deal with popular reactions to the Great Recession. We are already seeing it now with the protests in Greece, but also in Denmark and in a lot of other "civilized" European countries, where demonstrations are met with massive police forces sometimes accompanied by right-wing gangs that go out and help the police. That part of the current development of the state's response needs to be at the forefront of our minds when we try to assess the current situation.

The second element I find interesting is the contrast between this recession and the two that preceded it. The notion of "rollback neoliberalism" has been used to characterize the 1980s, while "rollout neoliberalism" has been used to characterize the 1990s, and currently leftist academics are not sure whether we should call it zombie neoliberalism, because it's still dominant even though it's dead. A lesson that we should keep in mind, based on the historical experience of the two previous crises, is that recessions can play a critical role in lowering the population's expectation of what they should expect from the economy. For instance, the 1981-1982 recession put an end to the idea of having one job for your life, while the 1991 recession accelerated this trend towards "flexibility" by adding globalization to the mix and cutting costs by moving work out of the developed countries into emerging nations. Offshoring first targeted just low-cost work, and then increasingly talent in IT and research and development was offshored to India and other countries. The current recession of 2008 can be interpreted as also opening up the opportunity for getting us used to things that people would have resisted otherwise. With what Naomi Klein would have called the "shock of a real crisis", the system keeps pressuring workers to give up everything that they have been struggling for in the last centuries, while some of the capitalists have to regroup and learn a couple of lessons. While mainstream media talk about how the talent of young students might no longer go into banking as much as it did, I think we should focus on the fact that unions will lose all of their historical achievements.

Finally, we may wonder what the Great Recession means for urban conflict and social movements. Of course, the media has it all wrong when they report on the burning of Greek cities and all over

Europe as the work of anarchist troublemakers. These actions are generally led by various organizations networked together and struggling against the current state of affairs by occupying embassies and attacking symbols of neoliberalism. There are connections between these different local movements, even though there is no top-down Obama-like machine telling the rank-and-file where to go. The question we need to ask ourselves is how these networked local movements can push the resistance further. We should keep in mind, in conclusion, that these movements and networks, in Greece and beyond, are often led by people representing both categories referred to by Peter Marcuse, namely the materially deprived and the culturally oppressed. The youth of today are both culturally oppressed and very much materially deprived, because in spite of their higher education they don't have decent job prospects at all, so it may be much easier to bridge the divisions between these two categories than it used to be in the Golden Age of Fordism.

David Harvey

My version of neoliberalism was that it was always about the restoration and consolidation of class power. Within that, there were all sorts of tactics and rhetoric which was largely a mystification of what was really going on. What was really going on was brilliantly revealed by William K. Tabb in his book about the long default of New York in which it became clear that the role of finance was crucial. The role of government was to support finance at all costs, and if there was a conflict between the well-being of financial institutions and the well-being of the people, you chose the financial institutions and you screwed the people. As Tabb pointed out, this kind of tactic, which worked in the New York Fiscal crisis, became the way in which the IMF then went out and did structural adjustment around the world, beginning in Mexico in 1982 and then all over the place ever since.

If you take that particular view of neoliberalism, then when you look at the bailout of the financial institutions you would say this is going on all over again. It's just bigger this time. Those eight guys came out of the room with a three-page document explaining why it was we had to give them 700 billion dollars, and one of them is the ex-head of Goldman Sachs and the other is the current head of what even the New York Times refers to now as Government Sachs. It seemed to me like we were actually living through a financial coup against the people of the United States. We should start to represent it in those terms. When you think about it in those terms, you see this massive amount of money flowing to the support of financial institutions, bailing them out. Yes, some of them are hurting, but as mentioned earlier what we are going to end up with is an incredible consolidation of class power.

In 1911 Andrew Melon said that in a crisis, assets return to their rightful owners. What this really means, and this is actually true about the whole history of capitalism, is that crises have not necessarily been about the destruction of capital. They have been about the reconfiguration of capital. In fact, crises are the irrational-rationalizers of the whole capitalist dynamic. We have to think about it in those terms in order to recognize that what's going on right now is the search for some irrational-rationalization so that class power is not going to be in any way challenged. It is going to be consolidated. We have to look at this crisis as not the end of anything but as the culmination and the next step along a particular line.

This has been going on since the 1970s. The issue in the late 1960s and 1970s in Europe and the US was indeed the question of labor organization, the question of labor scarcities, and all the rest of it. There were all sorts of ways in which means were explored as to how to deal with the labor question and the power of labor. Part of it was that technological change is a good way to do it, you could create unemployment that way. Another way is immigration. I remind you that with the reform of the Immigration Act in 1965, the US accessed the world's global labor force. In Europe for example, the Germans brought in the Turks, the French brought in the Maghrebians, and the Yugoslavs went to Sweden, all under state subsidy. There were all kinds of mechanisms.

If you couldn't do it that way, you off-shored. You took the stuff to China or the Maquila Zones, and there's a tremendous struggle over the labor issue there. If none of those technical means worked than you invented people like Reagan, Thatcher, and Pinochet who smashed the union movement and destroyed the power of labor. They then launched an incredible ideological campaign about freedom of the market, personal responsibility, and all the stuff we've been told is good for us about that particular kind of economy.

One of the consequences of this was that to the degree that the attack against labor won, by about 1980, the capitalist class was beginning to rake in very high profits. We've been through thirty years, in effect, of wage repression. That is, real wages haven't risen anywhere very much. Real wages have stagnated in the face of rising productivity. All of the benefits of this have gone to an increasingly smaller group in the capitalist class. Everybody knows about all of the incredible increases in inequality that have occurred and the tremendous amount of assets that have been accumulated by the top 0.1%.

What George Bush would say is that 'you need to give those people the money because they're the ones that are going to invest and reinvest in the economy.' But they don't. What they do is they invest in assets. They drive up asset prices. They invest in the stock market. The stock prices go up and they say, 'Oh, this looks like a good bet,' so they invest more in the stock market, so the stock market just goes up. And then, when the stock market goes down, they say, 'well let's look around somewhere else. Oh, the property market.' As asset values are driven up, it becomes very difficult for the rest of us that are not in that class to find someplace to live. The art market goes up, Picassos go up, and even the value of trophy wives goes up.

It is an interesting dilemma. This is a simple version of Marx, and it's not quite correct, but if you repress wages then you've got a problem in your market. Who are you going to sell your stuff too? I mean even Henry Ford realized it was important to have well-paid workers in order to sort your product. The only answer they could come up with is that you've got to get the working classes to borrow. The working class go into a massive indebtedness. You manufacture credit cards and lure people into a credit economy.

If you look at household indebtedness in the United States right now, you'd see it's three or four times what it was in 1980. Credit card debt is about ten times what it was in 1980. What you do is cover the gap between the production of value and the realization of value by having more and more people borrow. In effect, this puts the onus upon the financial institutions, and then the financial institutions start to operate at both ends of the cycle of capital. That is, they lend the money to people at the outset and then they lend money to people to purchase stuff at the end.

Take housing for example. You lend money to a speculative developer, they develop vast tracks of housing outside of San Diego. Then they say, 'my god we're going to lose all this money unless we can find someone to buy it, who the hell has money to buy it?' Well, no one has the money to buy it. Instead it is bought up with subprime mortgages and all the rest of it. I would call what is happening now a realization crisis of capitalism. It's a problem in the market. Therefore, I think that we're going to have an attempt to solve the problem by Keynesian strategy. You can see elements of that already emerging.

It seems that there are two difficulties. In this country, if you really want to launch a Keynesian strategy, one of the first things you'd have to do is re-balance the income inequalities. In other words, start engaging in the massive redistribution of wealth from the upper classes to the working classes. That would be absolutely essential. In fact, that's the only thing that worked in the Great Depression, particularly during and after World War II. That is what rescued capitalism then. Now, is Obama prepared to do that? What is that the Republican Party is saying about the bailout? They say smash the unions, nail them down. Obama is going to have a very hard time spreading the wealth around.

Even harder is that you can't launch a Keynesian strategy when you are so incredibly indebted that you cannot afford to go further into debt. The US is borrowing around 3 billion dollars a day in order to cover its indebtedness. To have a huge Keynesian program and borrow 5-6 billion dollars *a day*—where the hell is it going to come from? Are the Chinese going to give it to us? Are the Japanese going to give it to us? The only way you could launch a program of this kind, and at the same time do something about the deficit, is to cut military expenditures in half, get out of Iraq, not go into Afghanistan. The military budget would need to be savaged. Do you think Obama's going to do that? My God! The mess, the political outrage if you ever tried to do something like that. A real Keynesian strategy in this country is forestalled. It can't happen. The Chinese have the surpluses. They can recapitalize their banks and put in vast public work and employment programs. They're likely to do that for one very simple reason: the state of unrest in China. Particularly in the Pearl River Delta, where factories are closing down and massive unemployment is emerging. The Chinese are very nervous about the political consequences of such a policy, so they may engage in their own Keynesian strategy for their own kinds of reasons. They can do it. We can't.

I've mentioned the way in which asset prices get bid up. Since the 1970s there's been what I would call a capital surplus absorption problem. The more capital the capitalist classes got the less they could figure out what to do with it. Since the 1970s, how many financial crises have there been around the world? There have probably been around 40 or 50 of them. Then ask: how many of them were property market based? The answer is: a good 50% of them. The Swedish banking system went bankrupt in 1992 because of excessive speculation in property markets. The Japanese boom came to an end in the 1980s through excessive land and property speculation. In 1997 Asian Financial Crisis had a big property component to it. Again and again, you find these crises have a property base.

We should stop talking about the subprime mortgage crisis and talk about it as an urban crisis. If you look at foreclosures patterns you'll see the difference between Florida and California, which is defined by tracked housing or the new condominiums, and what's going on the older cities like Baltimore and Cleveland where there's been a financial Katrina effect. Whole neighborhoods have been completely wiped out, and it's almost always Hispanics or African American neighborhoods which have been completely destroyed. This has destroyed not only individual houses, but whole neighborhoods. We should be paying very close attention to the urban dynamic.

Now what does this mean when we bring it back to the Urban? The notion of the right to the city is one of the ways we can start to organize around a whole set of questions. For example, what to do in these semi-destroyed, in some cases totally destroyed, neighborhoods? What to do about people who have been displaced by this enlarged foreclosure movement?

There are some strategies which we can begin to think about. I would be in favor, for example, of campaigning nationwide to get municipalities to pass anti-eviction laws—just think what a difference that would make. Municipalities should be setting up housing corporations that can take over the foreclosed properties, can pay off the banks at 60 cents on the dollar and then allow people to have the continuous right to live in the place that they were living all along. In other words, we should start to looking at city charters that give the right to the continuity of residence, and actually attach the notion of citizenship to the notion of residence and, at the same time, secure residence. In order to do that, we have a huge ideological battle on our hands about private ownership. This idea that only owning property secures a right to the city needs to be attacked.

This brings me to the central problem. I think that the exit of the current crisis is already determined, it's prefigured, it's on its way. I can see various elements of that. This time, they cannot make it work as easily as they did in the past, because there is a serious legitimation crisis. How do you legitimate what is happening right now? The failure to deal with General Motors and, without any oversight whatsoever, giving billions of dollars to the financial institutions. How do you legitimize that? I think we are moving into the phase of a legitimation crisis. This is where people like us come in. We have a really acute role to play to emphasize it. That this system is about raw, naked class power located in the financial institutions. There are a few of them, they have immense power, and they can play all kinds of ideological games through the media. At the moment, the media is stuck trying to interpret everything in exactly the same terms as before. In other words, there's an attempt to say that nothing is really changing here, when actually things are changing.

It's at this particular moment that we have to be prepared to use words like 'capitalism,' and even 'socialism,' or 'communism.' We have to talk about socializing housing, education, and healthcare. We *have* to talk about those things. Now, how do you do it? In a centralized or decentralized way? How do you fund it? There are lots of questions to be asked, but we have to be prepared to talk about all of those issues. If not, what we're simply going to get coming out of this crisis is simply that they have prepared their axe, they are floating very nicely where they are—they've consolidated their class power. They're okay. Don't believe the stories, that just because one of these CEOs had to sell his art collection, they are running into hard times. They are not at all. There are some banks in this city doing beautifully right now, Lazard for example. For them, it's the best business years ever, because one of their skills is trying to value toxic assets. There's a very high demand for these services, and they're charging a very high premium for it. They're making out like bandits. These are things that we have to start confronting. They're doing fine, the rest of us are going to have to pay.

We should start doing what they're doing in Argentina, we should start occupying all these damn factories. We should start doing what they did in Buenos Ares, when the collapses occurred there, organizing whole neighborhoods around sustaining an economy of reciprocity in a situation of dire circumstances. Those are the things that have to start happening. We have to be prepared to talk about it in a way that is prepared fundamentally in response to Margret Thatcher's notion that there is no alternative. There goddamn better be one, or we're going to really make a mess of this world.

Neil Smith moderated this concluding panel on Radical Urbanism at the City University of New York Grad Center Conference on December 12, 2008.

"Radical Urbanism, The Right to the City, concluding panel," Youtube, last visited August 31, 2019, <https://www.youtube.com/watch?v=DkKXt6lTTD4&t=1229s>.

Building Democracy through Municipal Electoral Politics

Remembering Red Vienna

Veronika Duma and Hanna Lichtenberger

Though tragically snuffed out by the rise of fascism, Red Vienna was an island of socialist organizing and workers' power worth commemorating.

When it comes to progressive urban planning and municipal administration, "Red Vienna" (1919–1934) remains a common reference point. Best known for its housing programs, this radical municipal project also entailed comprehensive social improvements that included health care, education, child care, and cultural reform efforts.

Red Vienna represents a historically specific, social-democratic response to social and political questions that remain relevant today: the distribution of wealth, access to infrastructure, and the reorganization of reproductive labor. Against the backdrop of contemporary challenges to left, urban politics—the struggle for the right to housing, for public reinvestment, and against the rising right—we should look back on this sweeping interwar project to draw out the possibilities and limits of progressive urban politics within a conservative state.

Red Vienna's Social Basis

Other European cities also approved socially oriented, modernist housing projects for their urban working classes: both Frankfurt am Main ("New Frankfurt") and Zürich ("Red Zürich") initiated programs much like Vienna's in the wake of World War I, but none were nearly as expansive and ambitious.

The combination of social forces in Vienna at the end of and just after World War I created the necessary conditions for the project. Strong labor, feminist, and council movements emerged from the widespread hunger, unemployment, and homelessness that character-

60.000
sind's bisher,
80.000
sollen es werden!

SDAP's Election Campaign Poster, 1932 [Design: Siegfried Weyr]

ized the war years. These culminated in a wave of demonstrations and strikes toward the war's end. Throughout Vienna, workers and residents organized councils modeled on the Russian Revolution and the Council Republics in Germany and Hungary.

After the Austro-Hungarian monarchy collapsed, space for social transformation opened. In November 1918, the newly formed Austrian republic extended the vote to both women and men. This allowed the Social Democratic Worker's Party (SDAPÖ) to win the most votes in the first elections. The coalition government, consisting of the Social Democrats and the Christian Social Party (CS), which governed until 1920, introduced a series of progressive reforms that immediately improved workers' living conditions, such as the eight-hour day, paid vacation, the Works Council Act, the establishment of the Chamber of Labor, and rent-control legislation.

The nature of the SDAPÖ—which rested on the organizational integration of various radical and revolutionary currents—facilitated these programs. While some sections of the party negotiated with the opposition, they were able to use the pressure imposed by social movements to win additional concessions.[1] This history helps explain why the party still emphasizes unity. Unlike in Germany, Austria's SDAPÖ witnessed few major splits, and the Communist Party never—except during periods of illegality under the Austrofascists and the Nazis—established itself as a serious rival.

Socialists also organized outside of parliament through its military wing, the *Schutzbund*, and through the labor movement. In Vienna, the Social Democrats regularly won an absolute majority in city council elections, revealing that both the city's working class and large segments of the emerging white-collar professional class all gravitated toward the party. Red Vienna became a massive force in national politics.

But the challenges of running a socialist city within a conservative state soon became evident. The city administration pursued a political project that ran counter to the federal government's aims and, to some extent, even contrasted with the behavior of the more reformist wing in the Social Democratic Party.

Beginning in the 1920s, the balance of forces began to shift against the labor and women's movements' interests. Calls to eliminate the "revolutionary rubbish" grew increasingly loud in public debates. Following the collapse of the first governing coalition in 1920, the SDAPÖ would never again participate in a First Republic national government.

Meanwhile, as in Germany, inflation triggered by the war spread across the country. The currency's collapse only stopped after the League of Nations promised to guarantee foreign credits. The government planned to balance the national budget by raising revenue and cutting expenditures, a familiar formula that was, as always, conducted at the expense of the vast majority.

Red Urban Renewal

In Vienna, the SDAPÖ concentrated on municipal political projects. A thorough restructuring in all spheres of life, they thought, would produce the "new man" prepared for the coming socialist society. The approach's ideological foundation came out of Austro-Marxism, an ideology located somewhere between reform and revolution that sought to realize socialism through the ballot box. The corresponding political strategy emphasized building hegemony within the confines of the city.[2]

Vienna's municipal administration intervened in the postwar economic crisis with a massive investment and infrastructure program. Unsurprisingly, it immediately faced a barrage of criticism from bourgeois and right-wing forces. Opposition to Red Vienna's policies united the federal government, the main industrial and banking associations, big capital, the church, and the fascist and paramilitary organizations against the city.[3]

Despite internal and external resistance, the city council used a broad, tax-based wealth redistribution program to pay for the programs. This was only possible after 1922, when Vienna became a federal state and thus acquired far-reaching autonomy on tax policy. The Breitner tax, named after the councilor of finances, raised money from luxury goods and consumption, taxing cars, horse racing, and domestic servants. A progressive housing tax, which largely targeted villas and private homes while ignoring most working-class apartments, also supported the project.

The council created a broad economic stimulus program, including massive investments in infrastructure and job creation, while a wave of municipalization and nationalization swept the reproductive sector. The administration focused on spheres we would today describe as "care work"—nursing, medical care, education, and so on—and equipped them with improved infrastructure and significantly increased resources.

A massive expansion of child care and youth centers, modern nursing homes, and general health-care improvements followed. The administration pushed pedagogical reforms and increased opportunities for continuing education. Countless new libraries opened, often inside the public housing projects shooting up across the city. A broad network of publicly subsidized cultural associations and clubs gave more citizens access to cultural education. Together, these projects represented a comprehensive program of education reform and modernization. At the same time, new bridges, streets, parks, and promenades pushed forward the city's architectural reorganization.[456]

Decommodifying Shelter

In the nineteenth century, Vienna, as capital of the Austro-Hungarian Empire and residence of the Habsburg monarchy, grew into a metropolis of over two million inhabitants. In 1910, it ranked as the fifth-largest city in the world, after London, New York, Paris, and Chicago. Migrant labor from different parts of the empire allowed the city's industrial center to expand.

Much of the population lived in aging over-crowded apartment buildings without proper lighting and ventilation. Multiple generations crammed themselves into overpriced tenement blocks in the city's proletarian suburbs. Rents skyrocketed, and many lodgers only leased a bed between shifts at the factories. Tuberculosis as well as rickets—typical illnesses of the Viennese working classes—spread through the poorer districts.

The dire housing crisis following the war prompted the government to organize emergency housing, sometimes by expropriating vacant buildings. It opposed real estate speculation and successively bought up more and more property, so that by 1924 the Viennese government was the single largest property owner in the city. Between 1923 and 1934, it built over sixty thousand new apartments, which also served as job creators.[7] Further, the administration supported the settlement movement, in which homeless war veterans and other destitute individuals seized unused land and built houses on it.

Apartment complexes became the favored construction style, provoking the ire of the elites, who condemned the amount of money being spent on "red fortresses"—a label that points to the suspicion that they might someday serve military functions. When construction began on the Karl-Marx-Hof, a massive housing complex of roughly 1,400 units, many critics claimed it was structurally unsound. When the famous Amalienbad (a public natatorium in a working-class district) opened, the bourgeois press worried that proletarian visitors would steal its beautiful decorations.

These housing complexes were usually multistory apartment blocks with green inner courtyards that provided residents with natural light and strengthened community ties and solidarity. The city connected these blocks to local infrastructure—like consumer cooperatives and schools—making residents' daily lives easier by cutting down travel and shopping time.

The apartments themselves were generally about 125 and 150 square feet and consisted of an open-plan kitchen, one room, and sometimes an additional closet. All had running water and toilets.

Architects integrated the feminist and labor movements' demands into the building's layouts, and discussions around rationalizing and centralizing the domestic economy appeared in how the construction of the kitchens, child-care facilities, laundry rooms, and the *Einküchenhaus*—a series of apartment units served by one central kitchen. Planners intended that the state would take over traditionally female reproductive tasks and relieve women workers, already stressed by the triple burden of wage labor, housekeeping, and raising children.[8][9][10]

Neither the complexes nor the various companies and services established to support them were intended to make a profit. The city administration continued to run public services like gas, water, power plants, and public transportation and pushed to take over private industries including garbage disposal and the canals.

Rents were calculated to cover these operating costs and nothing more; in 1926, they averaged about 4 percent of a worker's monthly wage.[11] Apartment allocation was conducted according to a points system; alongside need, current housing situation, employment status, and war injuries, the city privileged applicants born in Vienna, which counted for four times as many points as Austrian citizenship.[12] This demonstrates the city's commitment to helping anyone who lived in the city remain there.

Nevertheless, beginning with the outbreak of the global economic crisis in 1929, Red Vienna came under increasing pressure, both economically and politically.[13]

The Socialist City in a Conservative State

The First Austrian Republic responded to economic crisis by pursuing a policy of austerity. Saving the state from the crisis required them to take out loans from the League of Nations, which came, of course, with strict conditions. League of Nations financial representatives travelled to Austria and developed a "restructuring program," which called for dismantling social infrastructure, cutting jobs, and slashing workers' rights. These policies were generally enforced via emergency decrees to avoid parliament and democratic decision-making more generally.

At the time, the labor movement press asked its readers a question that sounds eerily familiar over eighty years later: "Who will pay for the crisis?"

> *The crisis! Business people demand tax breaks, factory owners call for eliminating "social burdens." ... But is not the crisis felt ... first and foremost by those about whom no one speaks—by the workers, employees, and civil servants? Now more than ever! Because it is their wages they want to cut, their welfare costs, it is they who are to pay more taxes, so that direct taxation can be done away with ... In times of crisis, everyone is supposedly protected, only working people, and particularly women and the youth, are still forced to pay.*[14]

The government and League of Nations financial committee made no secret of the fact that they viewed democracy as disruptive and likely to endanger the program's success. So they established more authoritarian structures, justifying them by citing the country's dire economic need. The SDAPÖ criticized the austerity policies but nevertheless tolerated them at the federal level, at least in some instances. Red Vienna's destruction closely resembles the authoritarian neoliberal measures that have been implemented in the wake of the most recent crisis.[15] [16] At the same time, it highlights the limited power municipal governments have when confronted with externally imposed debt ceilings.

Over the course of the crisis, the bourgeois-conservative Austrian federal government increased pressure on Vienna's administration to cut expenses and increase revenues. While austerity was imposed at the federal level, the city tried to continue its investment programs, particularly with regard to apartment construction, albeit now on a smaller scale. Sessions of the city council were held "under the sign of frugality."

The Communist Party—not represented in parliament nor on the city council—had followed the Red Vienna project critically since its inception and protested these cutbacks, accusing the "Red City Council" of relieving the "ailing" economy at the expense of the "ailing" working class." On the federal level, the SDAPÖ proposed job creation programs and investments, as well as wealth redistribution through taxation, but their suggestions were ignored.

In February 1934, the Austrofascist government removed Vienna's administration in the course of its military evisceration of the labor movement as a whole, and appointed commissioners to rule the city. One of the caretaker government's first measures dismantled the progressive tax system. Redistribution of wealth from the top to the bottom reversed, public housing projects were largely abandoned, rents rose, and social insurance and infrastructure were dismantled.

Forgotten History, Forgotten Lessons

Reconsidering Red Vienna allows the contemporary left to build on these experiences and strategies. Although today's left has a vastly different character and exists in a very different political constellation, urban struggles continue. Anti-eviction movements (which include public-housing residents) and demands to productively use vacant space for new arrivals like refugees are mobilizing the Left across Europe. Red Vienna shows that far-reaching and transformational ideas can be made into reality, albeit in a specific situation in which massive pressure from below pushed through reforms.

Although today's Vienna feels the effects of gentrification and rising rents, the city maintains a relatively high public housing budget when compared to metropoles of similar size. Vital to the interwar reform project was a political force supported by large segments of the subaltern classes that opened up a space for further changes and transformations. At the same time, Red Vienna reminds us how important it is to address state power on local, national, and multiregional levels. While tax autonomy provided Red Vienna with greater room to maneuver, the city's progressive government could not defeat the combined forces of the national government and the League of Nations. At the time, the Austrian left dissected the SDAPÖ's strategy. Socialist, activist, and social scientist Käthe Leichter, later murdered by the Nazis, argued that the party's reluctance to address state power was its fatal mistake. The Left had lost "its faith in the creative power of the labor movement itself, the self-confidence in its own ability to act and shape society."[17]

We should take those lessons to heart, even while celebrating and defending the real achievements of socialist governance in Vienna.

Endnotes

1 Siegfried Mattl, "Wien im 20. Jahrhundert,"*Wien Perspektiven, Magazin für Linke Theorie und Praxis*, Summer 2010, 11.

2 Anson Rabinbach, *Vom Roten Wien zum Bürgerkrieg*, (Vienna,1989).

3 Emmerich Tálos and Walter Manoschek, 2005: "Zum Konstituierungsprozess des Austrofaschismus," in *Austrofaschismus. Politik–Ökonomie–Kultur 1933–1938*, ed. Emmerich Tálos and Wolfgang Neugebauer, (Münster:publisher, 2005), 6-27.

4 Helmut Weihsmann, *Das Rote Wien. Sozialdemokratische Architektur und Kommunalpolitik 1919–1934*, (Vienna:Promedia, 2002).

5 Inge Podbrecky, *Rotes Wien. Gehen & Sehen. 5 Routen zu gebauten Experimenten. Von Karl-Marx-Hof bis Werkbundsiedlung*, (Vienna, 2003).

6 Siegfried Mattl, "Wien im 20. Jahrhundert,"*Wien Perspektiven, Magazin für Linke Theorie und Praxis*, Summer 2010, 11.

7 Inge Podbrecky, *Rotes Wien. Gehen & Sehen. 5 Routen zu gebauten Experimenten. Von Karl-Marx-Hof bis Werkbundsiedlung*, (Vienna, 2003).

8 Helmut Gruber, "The 'New Women': Realities and Illusions of Gender Equality in Red Vienna,"in *Women and Socialism. Socialism and Women. Europe Between the Two World Wars*, edited by Helmut Gruber and Pamela Graves, (New York/Oxford: 1998), 56–94.

9 Gabriella Hauch, "Machen Frauen Staat? Geschlechterverhältnisse im politischen System," in *Frauen bewegen Politik. Österreich 1848–1938*, edited by Gabriella Hauch, (Innsbruck and others: Studienverlag, 2009), 151–170.

10 Gottfried Pirhofer and Reinhard Sieder, "Zur Konstitution der Arbeiterfamilie im Roten Wien. Familienpolitik, Kulturreform, Alltag und Ästhetik," in *Histor-

ische Familienforschung, edited by Michael Mitterauer and Reinhard Sieder, (Frankfurt and others: Suhrkamp, 1982), 326–369.

11 Inge Podbrecky, *Rotes Wien. Gehen & Sehen. 5 Routen zu gebauten Experimenten. Von Karl-Marx-Hof bis Werkbundsiedlung,* (Vienna: publisher, 2003).

12 Helmut Weihsmann, *Das Rote Wien. Sozialdemokratische Architektur und Kommunalpolitik 1919–1934,* (Vienna:Promedia, 2002).

13 Michaela Maier and Wolfgang Maderthaner, *Im Bann der Schattenjahre. Wien in der Zeit der Wirtschaftskrise 1929 bis 1934,* (Vienna: publisher, 2012).

14 Arbeiter-Zeitung, June 13, 1931, pp. 1-5.

15 Mark Blyth, *Austerity. The History of a Dangerous Idea,* (New York: Oxford University Press, 2003).

16 Veronica Duma and Katharina Hajek, "Haushaltspolitiken. Feministische Perspektiven auf die Weltwirtschaftskrisen von 1929 und 2008," in *Geld-Markt-Akteure, Österreichische Zeitschrift für Geschichtswissenschaften* edited by Oliver Kühschelm (Innsbruck and others: Studienverlag, 2015) 46–76.

17 Anson Rabinbach, *Vom Roten Wien zum Bürgerkrieg,* (Vienna 1989).

The FRAP (Political Action Front) 1970–1974: The First Experience of Radical Municipalism in Montréal

Donald Cuccioletta

Right to the City and the Thirst for Change

For the past 20 years or so there has been a renewed interest in municipal politics, germinating from the grassroots. Cities have become large urban centers, where capitalist interests have converged to create a monopolized space over the territory in which most people on our planet live. The United Nations study on sustainable cities stated:

> Since 2007, more than half of the world's population has been living in urban areas and the figure is estimated to exceed 70 percent by 2050. This is a hallmark of the transformation of humans' economic base and social structure, in as much as, previously populations lived and worked primarily in rural areas.[1]

In 2006, the capitalist system had precipitated its latest crisis. Today, we are in the process of reconstructing and reconfiguring the capitalist system through the manipulation of cities and large urban centers. The concentration of banks, financial institutions, real estate corporations, post-industrial companies, research centers (including artificial intelligence), the invasion of condominiums, the destruction of human urban space and the air we breathe, all of this in the name of capitalist materialism. The rise of vast urban development projects, where people have become secondary in the new definition of the city (e.g. the Royalmount Project in Montréal), are a good example of the inner-city destruction in the name of capitalist profit. Nevertheless, this struggle is not new for those who have made the city the target of their class struggle.

Amid the May 1968 confrontations in Paris, Henri Lefebvre put forward the idea of the "Right to the City."[2] In this seminal work, which has become the manifesto for the radical activists of city politics,

Lefebvre examined the role and the importance of the city in the structure of capitalism. He clearly placed the city at the pivotal center of the jungle that is capitalism. Cities, for him, had become the central block from which capitalism would pursue and spread its exploitive system. In essence, Lefebvre launched a new ideology within the concept of "class struggle" and placed the city at the center of the destruction of capitalism. But Lefebvre would not be alone in this analysis.

Peter Marcuse, a renowned urban theorist, took up the mantle laid by Lefebvre and pursued the question of the "Right to the City." Marcuse applied it to urban theory in order to produce a practical organizational approach for citizens to apply, and eventually, to take the city. As Marcuse writes, "focusing on the difference of 1968, which produced the demand for the Right to the City, and the crisis we confront today. The question then is: how do we understand the Right to the City today, and how can a critical urban theory contribute to implementing it?"[3] Today's crisis of the city should not be interpreted strictly in terms of the general theory of neo-liberalism, characterized by austerity measures fostered by the financial capitalist system, but should be understood in the context of the concrete consequences of exploitation, domination, and oppression that exist throughout the capitalist system. We should examine how this is embedded in the cities of today.

To concretely expose these elements and how they affect the cities of today remains the principle necessity of a popular education directed towards the citizens who inhabit these cities. The 2008 financial crisis, which is still felt today in many countries, has produced for the capitalistic class a new set of parameters to be applied to cities and urban centers in order to maintain the profit system and the expansion of its imperialistic twin.

The cities today have become the focal point for the reconstruction of capitalism and imperialism: the concentration of banks and financial institutions, land speculation, environmental and ecological issues, massive urban projects, lack of affordable housing, transportation issues, urbanization, and the race for profit. The major issues that the world is grappling with are concentrated in the cities where, as mentioned, more than half of the world's population has lived since 2007.

We now see that the idea of the Right to the City and the theory of radical municipalism are being fostered in neighborhoods through a revival of citizen committees. Because of this renewed interest in radical municipalism, the history and analysis of the Montréal-based *Front d'action politique* (FRAP) has become a focal point of interest. Was the FRAP born out of the ideas of Henri Lefebvre? Were there other influences? What was the political basis for founding the FRAP? With social upheaval attributed to the Québec "Quiet Revolution", which we will get more into in the following section, the University of Montréal felt the need not only to develop their sociology department but also to expand programs towards social work in the neighborhoods throughout the cities and rural areas of the province of Québec. This was a major breakthrough for social science, and it recognized the need to develop social workers who actually intervened in housing issues, poverty, the lack of democracy for citizens, and the exploitive system in general. This new cohort of social workers were more interested in class-oriented solutions rather than traditional ones. In their university studies, part of their curriculum was the study of Saul Alinsky. He believed in a grassroots, neighborhood-based approach to the struggle. Alinsky was, in many ways, the grandfather of the FRAP. Hence, these newly trained social workers and sociologists transformed and integrated their university approach of social practice into a more pragmatic and class struggle-oriented approach. These new graduates moved to cities across Québec as well as rural towns and villages that had been forgotten with the thrust towards industrialization and modernity in the cities. The rural areas abandoned by the provincial government were left to fend for themselves.

In the rural areas this gave rise to a pan-provincial movement called *Les indignés* (The Indignants). This movement was in many ways similar to the contemporary group of *Los Indignados* in Spain, who eventually gave rise to the Podemos political party. We must remember, Québec's development from the early colony of New France was always dominated by rural industries of mining, lumber, and agriculture. But with the major changes precipitated by the Quiet Revolution, the rural areas and the above-mentioned industries were left abandoned due to a lack of modern methods, innovation, and finance. People left their villages and small towns for the cities because of a lack of work—a forced migration.

These activists and social workers in the rural areas gave birth to grassroots organizations which fostered input in the development of a movement for social and political change. Rural areas were not to be forgotten for the role they played in the history of Québec. Sometimes these changes were progressive—Les idigniés—and sometimes they were regressive—the National Union Party[4] of the past and the Coalition Avenir Québec (CAQ) today.

Since the Confederation of 1867, the year that Canada became an independent nation-state and Québec an official province within it, the rural areas were dominated by the Catholic Church. The Church preached total obedience to the Catholic doctrine of large families (16 children on average) and low-wage subservient labour. In addition to the control of the Catholic Church, Québec society was also dominated by the reactionary policies of the National Union Party founded and led by Maurice Duplessis.

Maurice Duplessis governed from 1936 to 1940 and then from 1944 to 1958. The party was guided by a philosophy of free-market capitalism, which was based on a culture of conservatism characterised by an openness to American investment and control that rejected unionism and anti-left parties (particularly the communists). This period under Duplessis was given the name by future historians as "La Grande noirceure" (the great darkness). With the sudden death of Maurice Duplessis in 1958, the subsequent leaders could not maintain the leadership of the party over Québec society. The Union National was a party founded by Maurice Duplessis and over the years in power had become his own personal party. His sudden death caught the party by surprise and heralded the beginning of a new era in Québec.

The Québec Quiet Revolution: A Noisy Evolution

The FRAP did not appear suddenly and out of nowhere. It was a long process of urban social struggles led by grassroots citizens groups in the diverse neighborhoods of Montréal. As alluded to previously, the Maurice Duplessis regime under the Unione Nationale party, supported by the Catholic Church, the French-Canadian bourgeoisie, and the English-Canadian bourgeoisie in Québec imposed a program of conservative politics that kept Québec and its working classes underdeveloped compared to the rest of Canada and North America. This did not bode well with the English Canadian bourgeoisie in the rest of Canada. Québec was lagging behind economically, generating low profits for the English-Canadian bourgeoisie. Change had to happen in Québec.

The Québec Liberal party, in an alliance with the English-Canadian bourgeoisie, took power in 1960, The election was won under the slogan *"Il faut que ça change"* (It has to change). From 1960 to 1962, several reforms were put in place in order for Québec and its economy to perform in accordance with national standards. The introduction of Keynesian-style state intervention in the economy was the major administrative policy introduced by Québec's Liberal Party in the legislative assembly.

Rising high in the polls, another election was called in 1962 under the slogan *"maître chez nous"* (masters of our own house). A nationalist slogan for sure, but not surprising because the nationalist movement in Québec had been growing since the end of World War II and the Liberal Party of Québec always had a nationalist wing within the party. A massive victory for the Liberal party heralded in more major reforms that comprised the political and social basis of the Quiet Revolution.

There was the nationalization of electricity into the then existing Hydro Québec, led by René Lévesque Minister of Natural Resources and Eric Kierans Minister of Finance and the first Department of Education under the stewardship of Paul Gerin Lajoie was put in place. Thus began the total reform of Québec's education program under the Parent Commission led by Guy Rocher, the most prominent sociologist in Québec at that time. Up until the Quiet Revolution, the school system had been managed by the Catholic Church and the Archbishop of Québec City in accordance with the Québec Act of 1774. The teachers were priests, brothers, or nuns. Similarly, with the state takeover of hospitals, the government instituted nursing schools and replaced the nuns who had served as nurses. Meanwhile, measures were taken to develop a universal healthcare system, which was fully implemented in 1970. The Department of International Relations, inspired by the report of Paul Painchaud, was put in place and eventually sent Québec delegations across the world. This, and much more, was done within the relatively short period of four years. This was the essence of Québec's Quiet Revolution.[5]

These fundamental changes, which transformed Québec society, gave the working-class, labour unions, citizens, and progressives a sense that this was a revolutionary period which had to go beyond governmental and state institutions. Québec labour unions and progressives were well aware of the National Liberation movements that led anti-colonial and anti-imperialistic struggles throughout the third-world. Progressives, and the minority of Marxists, anarchists, and communists celebrated the Algerian Revolution and, a few years later, the Cuban Revolution. Similarly, the same progressives were against the Vietnam War, condemned American imperialism, and many assisted in bringing draft-dodgers north to Canada and Québec.

The Québec Quiet Revolution had opened the floodgates for change. The subsequent wave of change benefited from the opening of Québec society, not just in the infrastructure of government but also in Québec society in general. Many of the early activists of the left, who led the struggle against the autocratic regime of Duplessis supported by a newly-awakened generation, led the charge for social transformation. The political effervescence of this period had reached the street level in the neighbourhoods of Montréal and in other cities around the province. Popular culture, as defined by Antonio Gramsci, became an instrument of social change in Québec.

Very quickly into the first three years of the Quiet Revolution, social activists and nationalist elements began intervening with expectations of major changes in Québec society. Expectations were very high for most people. For most members of Québec society, change was not simply seen as modernizing government infrastructures.

In 1963, the first wave of the Front de libération du Québec (FLQ) began, a group that believed acts of terrorism against Québec's enemies was necessary to stimulate and awaken the Québec masses to necessary social and national change. Originally composed of university intellectuals, bombs were placed in various postal boxes which still had British symbols on them to send the message that Québec was still under the yoke of the English. They believed that Québec needed independence from Canada, a country under British rule. In 1964, the Queen of England, Elizabeth II came to Québec City as a symbol of Britain's attachment to Canada. The Samedi de la matraqueriots (Truncheon Saturday) ensued and marked Québec's contemporary history. The Queen never revisited Québec even though she and her royal family visited the rest of Canada on many occasions.

The first wave of the FLQ was based on a nationalist ideology, while the second (led by Pierre Paul Geoffroy) and third waves (led by Vallières and Gagnon) were a mixture of socialist ideas within the national context of a Québec liberation movement. The fourth wave resulted in the events of the October Crisis. The FLQ was supported by most radicals but was rejected by the majority of Francophones in Québec.

This period was also marked by momentous, violent demonstrations that energized the citizens' social movement. The demonstrations which demanded the release of Pierre Vallières and Charles Gagnon—who were being held in prison in New York City on charges of disturbing the peace in front of the United Nations—Québec independence, and the release of all political prisoners held in Québec gave the international spark necessary for independence and social movements. Pierre Vallières and Charles Gagnon became household names and were actually seen as social heroes within Québec's radical circles.

A strike led by the Confédération des syndicats nationaux (CSN; Confederation of National Trade Unions) and the Fédération des travailleurs et travailleuses du Québec (FTQ; Québec Federation of Labour), which demanded a union contract written in French against the 7-Up bottling plant in the Town of Mount Royal, sparked a series of demonstrations that would come to define Québec's political and social scene in 1968. Supported by various groups in the social movement, the strike also drew the support of the Rassemblement pour l'indépendance nationale (RIN; Rally for National Independence), founded by Pierre Bourgault and L'Union générale des étudiants du Québec (UGEQ; the Québec Student Union).

The 7-Up strike of 1968 culminated in a series of massive demonstrations that rocked Québec, and particularly Montréal, in 1968 and 1969. The St. Jean Baptiste parade, with Prime Minister Trudeau in attendance, was followed by a massive demonstration led by the Front de libération du Québec (FLP; Popular Liberation Front). Trudeau was pelted with rocks. The demonstration in Québec against Bill 63—proposed by the Union Nationale party— would have weakened the French language in Québec as the dominant language. The violent Murray Hill demonstration held in downtown Montréal led to gunfire and to Operation McGill Français in 1969, organized by the FLP and numerous other popular groups around Montréal, which attempted to force McGill University to break down the wall of segregation and to accept Francophone students.

Meanwhile, in the working-class neighborhoods of Montréal, *groups populaires* (people's groups) were founded to confront the various struggles faced by the working-class. In many working-class neighbourhoods, anglophone workers were an important cohort and helped encourage integrated popular groups established by francophones.[6] Participation in multiple confrontational actions led to a growing social movement put together by grassroots organizations led by the working-class. This was not the era of community groups feudalized by the State, as is the case today.[7] These women and men of the working class saw the need to protest and organise as necessary to improve their daily lives.

Citizen committees emerged in every neighborhood. Women's groups were formed, and eventually the Mouvement de libération des femmes (MLF; Women's Liberation Movement) was founded. Some of these groups went on to establish public daycare centers, which was a first in Québec and Canada. Housing was always a problem; Montréal had a renter majority, then and now. *Committees de logement* (housing committees) were formed and people's health clinics were established, the most famous was in the working-class neighbourhood of Point St. Charles. These health clinics became critical for the future of Québec's Centres locaux de services communautaires (CLSC; Local community services centres).

Québec's community-led food cooperatives were a crucial development. In French they were called *comptoir alimentaire*. Established primarily in working-class neighbourhoods, they were controlled by the workers, both women and men of the neighbourhood, and served the needs of the poor and low-income working-class. The food, bought and sold at-cost, was of very good quality and was controlled by the various committees within the co-op. All the work within the co-op was done by the members and organized by general assemblies. These food co-ops were at the center of the struggle against the high cost of living. The housing committees in each neighbourhood forged alliances with these food co-ops to fight the high cost of living in terms of food and rents.

A special mention needs to be said about citizens in Milton Parc who, with the guidance of Lucia Kowaluk and Dimitrios Roussopoulos, initiated the struggle for cooperative housing on a large-scale, comprising many city blocks. Milton Parc citizens organized and engaged in a long-lasting battle to prevent a massive urban redevelopment in the area characterised by high towers and luxury apartments. Today the name of Milton Parc is synonymous with battles for cooperative housing throughout North America.

The importance of these different citizen groups in creating the beginning of a vast social movement forced the working-class to take a much closer look at the politics of the city. This work sent a message to community organizers and social workers on the ground, to develop a series of popular education classes in the various working-class neighbourhoods called Citoyen face au Pouvoir (Citizens confronting power). The power referred to was municipal, provincial, and federal power. But the emphasis in these popular educations classes was put on municipal power. Why?

There were two developments that helped to enmesh the social movement and the idea of municipal politics as a future strategy to implement. First, many of the people's groups were interacting together across neighbourhood lines. The need to meet, exchange, compare strategies, and create solidarity within the common struggle began to appear. Some of the strategies put in place were similar and some were not. Therefore, the need for interactive strategies was felt on the municipal level and led to a strategic solidarity among the different groups in the neighborhoods.

The second development—which was heralded by the social movement, the labor unions, activists for a wider democracy, and the citizens of all cities and towns across Québec—was a law passed by the Union Nationale government in 1968, which gave the right to vote to every citizen in municipal elections with the presentation of proof of residency in the said town or city. Elected democracy had arrived in the cities and the towns of Québec. These two developments sparked discussions about the possibility of creating a unified municipal movement in Montréal.

Another factor that must be included in this period was the significant attention that radical activists in Québec gave to the events May 1968 in Paris. We felt like we were part of a vast movement interconnected by the same struggles. Other important groups and events in the United States—such as Berkley, the Black Panthers, the Stonewall riots, and the protests at Democratic National Convention in Chicago (at which this author was a participant)—were followed religiously by radical forces in Québec.

The FRAP: A First for Municipal Radicalism in Montréal.

The FRAP was the first attempt at radical municipalism in Québec. It did not develop in a political vacuum nor did it fall from the heavens. It is clear that it was a product of the political revolution that went beyond the intentions of the Québec Quiet Revolution. It was also a product of the class-struggle that was taken up by many activists, radical groups, labour unions, and the student movement, which led to the emergence of a broad, radical social movement. This had never been seen before in Québec history, let alone in the city of Montréal.

In 1968 the most radical labour union in Québec at that time, the CSN, under the leadership of then President Marcel Pepin, forged ahead to create a policy approved by the membership of the CSN which lead to the direct political action named Le deuxième front (The Second Front). Besides maintaining its trade union policies of negotiations, union contracts, strikes, grievance procedures, the CSN decided to enter the arena of politics. The thinking behind this new policy was that we could not leave it to the government or the capitalist classes to resolve the problems of the working class. Labour unions, in this case the CSN, had to get involved in the process of political power. This not only energized unionized workers across Québec but also the labour movement in general. In Montréal, this led the local labour council of the CSN to focus on municipal politics and to take power in Montréal.

Working-class people in the neighbourhoods saw Le deuxième front policy as an opportunity to incorporate the CSN into the municipal struggle. It went without saying that the policy of Le deuxième front was instrumental in forming Montréal's municipal movement. All knew well that money was needed to enter electoral politics. Le deuxième front not only meant a political step forward but it also sent the message to all citizens groups that the CSN was willing to support the municipal movement with a budget. The question which remained was how to fuse the labour movement in Montréal, under the CSN, with the citizen movements represented by the various popular groups throughout the different neighborhoods.

The first step by the citizen activists was to reassemble all of the various groups with a common platform. The Regroupment d'action politique (RAP; Political Action Grouping) was formed, it was based on localised activism and taking control of the neighborhoods. But it was also a first step towards a political party totally committed to taking the city. This was not an easy task. Many of the citizens groups were skeptical of being dominated by both the large labor union of the CSN and a top-down political party on the municipal scene. They had heard all the promises of the traditional bourgeois parties of the past. Therefore, the first question that had to be answered was how was a new municipal political party, one based on the citizen groups in the neighborhoods, would be different from all other traditional bourgeois parties of the past. The second question was how we could guarantee full control by citizen groups in their respective neighborhoods? In order words, how could we have a working model for the neighborhoods to be in control of municipal and local democracy?

The proposed solution to these very legitimate questions put forward by working-class citizens in the neighborhoods was the FRAP Manifesto (included in the Annex of the book). A steering committee was formed with representatives from the different neighborhoods who had the task of producing such a manifesto. The different community organisers working in the neighborhoods were also members of the committee. It was from these community organisers that the ideas of Sol Alinsky filtered to the grassroots level.

The FRAP Manifesto was a first in Québec and Canada. It attempted to outline a working-class program directed towards neighborhood democracy characterized by citizen control. It is not perfect, but it was a working-class document that was relevant then and now. It was entitled "Le sens de notre action" (The Sense of our Action).[8]

The introduction attempted to reflect the working-class struggle. With subtitles such as "Workers' are excluded from power" and "A Popular movement is on the rise."[9] Though these subtitles referred to a Marxist approach to struggle, this did not necessarily mean that the FRAP was a Marxist organization. Yes, there were Marxist members at different levels of involvement, just as there were citizens in the different popular groups who were Marxists, anarchists, social democrats, PQ, labor activists, and leftist in general. At that time there was a document circulating within the popular groups that used Marxism as a guide to analyze capitalist society. The FRAP was part of the Marxist trend developing within the CSN, the FTQ, and the intellectual circles and citizens groups throughout Montréal and Québec.

The ultimate goal of the FRAP was to eventually win a municipal election and put in place a working-class, bottom-up democracy controlled by the citizens in each respective neighborhood of Montréal. However, the immediate goal was to expose the Drapeau-Saulnier municipal administration who were, as all municipal administrations, feudalized to the banks, financial institutions, business class and the bourgeois elites of the city.[9] The FRAP also wanted to elect a few municipal council representatives who would become the opposition to city hall and begin to expand popular political education.

In the 60s and early 70s, the FRAP prioritized "Popular Power." This slogan came out of Mai'68 Paris where the idea of *pouvoir populaire*, born from the writings of Henri Lefevbre, made its way across the Atlantic and was taken up by the militant activists in the working-class neighborhoods of Montréal. This was the centerpiece of the popular education movement for the working class. The FRAP was not founded for a one electoral win, but was seen and founded for the long process of organising a city around working-class demands.

The cornerstone of the FRAP was the comités d'action politique (CAP; political action committees). The CAP was, according to the FRAP Manifesto,[10] to be the political voice of the people, from the popular groups, the labor committees in the neighborhoods, and the students. The CAP was the pivotal force in the neighborhoods that directed the political messaging of the FRAP. When we combine these targeted groups, the CAP was able to reach the working class, the poor, the lower middle class, and the progressive elements in the middle class.

The CAP also had three main goals that formed its political platform in the neighborhoods. The most important was to establish the idea of an urban democracy, which we would call today direct citizen democracy. Secondly, it was to develop the opportunity for citizens to participate in the city's political life. And thirdly, fostering a working-class unity without which none of the above could be achieved.

The CAP was an organization based on struggle. Its approach was pragmatic, directly involving citizens with popular education to promote rights. It focused on the three main issues that exploited and oppressed citizens in their neighborhoods. The first issue was the idea of consumption, related to the cost of living. Housing, health, food, and credit had been central concerns for many citizen groups. Montréal has always been a renter's city. In the working-class neighborhoods, the majority of landlords at that time were absentee landlords, who imposed abusive rents and maintained shabby flats and apartments. The CAP advocated for developing cooperative housing (i.e. Milton Parc) and the takeover of the administrative boards of the local *caisse populaire* (credit unions),[11] where most francophone workers put their savings.

In the working-class neighborhoods of Montréal, such as Maisonneuve, large companies like Canadian Vickers and CPR Angus Shop dotted the landscape. Many of the workers were employed in these factories and lived in the same neighborhoods. The working-class labor and union struggles spilled from the factories into the neighborhoods in which they were based. The CAP, as a second front, participated in these labor and local struggles. In Maisonneuve, when workers at Canadian Vickers went on strike, the CAP supported them by printing and distributing flyers.

The main front, in the long term, was political education. The FRAP was a working-class party and as such it was distinct from the traditional bourgeois parties that existed only to defend capitalist interests. The education front was very challenging. The CAP had to deconstruct the years of alienation and bourgeois propaganda that made the workers believe that all these municipal parties were there for the workers good. This remains difficult today. But it is the type of activism that was expected of the CAP.

The biggest challenge for the FRAP was to show concretely that it was the complete opposite of the traditional bourgeois parties who had dominated City Hall since Confederation. There had to be a distinct break with the past that would be recognizable to ordinary people. This hurdle had to be overcome to prove that the FRAP Manifesto was more than an accumulation of nice and catchy slogans. Actions had to speak louder than words.

In order to run a campaign, and hopefully take power, you needed candidates to run for your party. At that time, we were still believers in representative liberal democracy. Therefore, the task was to find candidates to run for the FRAP. Electoral districts had been created along the lines of the existing neighborhoods and were divided into three wards. Each CAP had to find three candidates, and in some cases four depending on the division of the neighborhood, to run for the FRAP. With the election scheduled for November, the race was on.

The general assemblies of the CAP were open to the public and especially to the neighborhood citizen groups. Nominations were put forward for the candidates that were considered the most capable of representing the working-class composition of the neighborhood. Many individuals were proposed, but only a small number of women.[12]

In Maisonneuve, three candidates were selected and the CAP was charged to meet with each proposed candidate to hear their vision for the upcoming election. There was a dock worker of the Port of Montréal, a student who had been a long-time activist in the citizens committees, and an unemployed construction worker who had work to set up a food coop in the borough.

From our election headquarters, citizens gave their time and energy to canvas their designated areas, handing out flyers, organising public meetings by street, and putting forward three candidates and the FRAP Manifesto. Hopes were high, maybe too high.

The local election headquarters was broken into on numerous occasions by what we still believe was the police, to the steal names of the election workers, and compile dossiers for future intimidation. Members and sympathizers of the FRAP were well aware that we were going up against the bourgeois powers that be. CAP Maisonneuve, its members, and its sympathizers never gave up. As the election went forward, more people joined to help. All these actions were a first for over 90% of the citizens involved. We can now see that the FRAP Manifesto and its electoral program had resiliency within the working class.

The position taken by the leadership committee was to present municipal candidates in all the electoral districts, but not to present a mayoral candidate. The analysis was that Jean Drapeau was too strong to defeat as a returning mayor. Drapeau had been elected for the first time in 1954 to 1957 and from 1960 to the present 1970 election, which he won with over 75% of the vote all the 52 municipal council seats. He went on to win every election until 1986. The need was to take the municipal council and create an active opposition, to continue to propagate participatory democracy and the FRAP Manifesto. Thirty-two candidates were chosen and they received 18.5% of the vote.

These results were extraordinary considering the fact that the election was held under the application of the War Measures Act that had been enacted by the federal government of Canada. Over 1,500 homes across Québec were raided and hundreds were arrested and held in custody from a few days to four months. Montréal and the FRAP were living under martial law. This was the October Crisis.

Two candidates of the FRAP, Henri Bellemare in St. Jacques and Jean Roy in St Louis, were arrested and held by the Provincial Police. Many organizers were arrested and held in local police stations across Montréal. Many other organizers were followed and photographed by the Royal Canadian Mounter Police (RCMP). The election workers were followed during their neighborhood canvassing by components of the Canadian Army, RCMP, SQ and Montréal Police. FRAP election workers were insulted and spit on by reactionary forces supporting the Drapeau-Saulnier Administration. Considering the circumstances that surrounded this election, 18.5% of the popular was a victory for democracy in times when there was no democracy.

Analytical Reasons for the Demise of the FRAP

It was obvious that the October crisis killed the spirit of the FRAP. You sensed the disarray in the subsequent meetings of the CAPs and the elected permanent council. There was no ideological response that could have explained the defeat despite the 18.5% win by the FRAP. The FRAP did support the goals of the 1970 FLQ, but settled on a more democratic approach for social change. Of course, the bourgeois reactionaries jumped on the occasion to accuse, as did Jean Marchand, Minister of labor in the Pierre Trudeau cabinet, that the FRAP was political front of the FLQ, similar to the relation between Sinn Fein and the Irish Republican Army.

Attempts to solidify the FRAP for future elections failed as many of the CAPs, especially CAP Maisonneuve and CAP St-Jacques (considered the most radical) left the organization. By 1973, the FRAP was a shell of its former self and it quietly disbanded. The general assumption by the majority of its members was that the FRAP was the victim of the October Crisis. But this was not the end of the subsequent analysis done by certain CAPs to dig deeper and to learn the numerous reasons for the disappearance of the FRAP.

There is no question that the demise of the FRAP was caused by the October Crisis of 1970. Never had the activists at that time experienced the full imposition of a fascist policy that was the War Measures Act. This young generation of activists, born out of the swift changes brought about by the Quiet Revolution, had never lived and even understood the meaning of the presence of the Canadian army in the streets of Montréal.

Of course some of the older members of the FRAP like Michel Chartrand (CSN member) and Fernand Boudreault (FTQ member) had experienced similar situations with the Asbestos Strike of 1948 and Murdockville of 1954, when Maurice Duplessis ordered the Provincial Police (in many ways his own private police force) armed with automatic weapons to raid homes across Québec in search of labor activists and communists. But this new generation of 20-year olds had never experienced something of this nature. The author had experienced Chicago in 1968, but this paled in comparison to the October Crisis. We were scared and this was normal.

Not knowing how to respond politically and ideologically to this massive oppression left the FRAP with no counter attack. The FRAP and its young militants ran an election under the presence of fascism. This demonstrated that, even though the majority believed they were of the left, the question was which left. What was our central ideology, besides contesting a municipal election that would hold us together come hell or high water?

The membership split on this debate. CAP Maisonneuve and CAP St. Jacques felt that we needed to adhere to a unified radical ideology while others preferred a more social democratic approach in tune with the newly founded PQ. Throughout these internal debates, the leadership, including the labor representatives on the leadership council, moved towards a position referred to as "Independence and then socialism," which had been voiced by the so-called left of the PQ. While the younger generation, heavily influenced by Paris'68 and the radical movements in the United States, followed a more radical line—with the birth of new Marxist groups such as Mobilisation, Mouvement révolutionnaire des étudiants du Québec (MREQ), Noyaux des petites enterprises (NPE) in Maisonneuve district, Cellule militante ouvrière (CMO), and Cellule ouvrière révolutionnaire (COR)—70% of the members had already left the FRAP. CAP St.

Jacques was behind the emergence of the COR. CAP Maisonneuve was instrumental in forming the NPE. The FRAP could not survive this debate, which was pivotal moving forward in the struggle against capitalism, even on the municipal level.

The FRAP was a social democratic approach which for its time was a vast step forward, but we learned very quickly that when you confront the bourgeoisie and the capitalist state, social democracy was not steeped enough in the idea of class struggle in order to respond to fascist tactics.

Of the 32 candidates that ran in the election only 3 were women. In the leadership council, and in all of the CAPs, the leadership was 90% male. Yet, in most of the popular groups in which the working-class districts were founded, groups were administered and led by a vast majority of women. The housing committees, the health committees, the citizens committees, the food coops, and the newly formed daycares, were formed and led by women. Women took care of social issues, but the domain of politics still belonged to men. This was a major weakness of the FRAP and one that this author believes was a major failing that led to the demise of the FRAP.

Women stood firm in their criticism to the way the organization functioned. Women in Québec had begun the feminist struggle in the mid-sixties (Le Front de liberation des femmes was formed in 1968) but it was very obvious that men, especially within the FRAP, still projected a chauvinistic vision of class struggle.

The organizational structure of the FRAP attempted to give more room to the grassroots.[13] However, the conceptual framework was still dominated by the vertical approach of the top-down. It was true that the concept of a horizontal approach had not been conceived or even talked about in the 60s and even the 70s. Many of the popular groups—particularly women's groups who already felt pushed aside—led the fight for more democratic participation. The struggle for a more democratic structure for the FRAP, was part of a new feminist approach to society in general.

Those who are still with us, and those who lived the experience of the FRAP as an attempt to instill a radical municipalism for Montréal, have remained involved in new movements that have taken up the torch for class struggle to "Take the City."

Conclusion: The Renaissance of Municipal Radicalism

There seems to be a return to the focus on the cities. Since the capitalist crisis began in 2006, many of the analyses regarding the restructuring of capitalism have centered on the role of cities. In Montréal, civil society has redirected its focus to the rule of the city, with growing numbers of citizen committees. The problems mentioned in the FRAP Manifesto still remain. The hardships of the working class, the poor, and the lower middle class are still prominent.

A new generation of activists has arisen which sees the city as a center of class struggle. The cities of today have become the centerpiece of the struggle against climate change. Activists and authors such as Jonathan Durand-Folco have written about a renewed role of the city, while mentioning the history of the FRAP. A resurgence to the writings of David Harvey and Dimitrios Roussopolous—who have, over the years, been beacons of ideas on the city—are educating a new generation.

Colloquiums on grassroots organizing have emerged. Citizens have returned to recognize that the city, especially the city they live in, is central to their social and political wellbeing. But the idea of radical municipalism in the form of direct citizen (women and men) democracy, citizen control over their neighborhoods, the need for grassroots organisation and not necessarily a party structure, of a horizontal vision of political power, political and social ecology, LGBTQ citizens as an integral part of a city's population, etc. still has to be the basis of a new focus on popular education.

The rise of new organizations, such as the Montréal Urban Left among others, are signs that activists have returned to the fold of "Taking the City." Much work has to be done in reuniting the working class, the poor, the lower middles class, labor activists, neighborhood organizers, and activists in general, not necessarily under the wing of an organization but more to instill by a return to popular education the idea of the "Right to the City."

We have been witnesses to how social democratic and social technocratic rhetoric, once in power, serve to cloud the political landscape in favor of bourgeois politics and control. An attempt to popularize the political and ideological idea of the "Right to the City" in

Montréal may be a return to the contemporary history of the FRAP and the FRAP Manifesto with its successes and failures. This could help to reenergize a radical leftist approach to the city as a center for system change.

THE RIGHT TO THE CITY/LEDROIT À LA VILLE
TAKE THE CITY/PRENONS LA VILLE

Endnotes

1 See United Nations Study (2015), *Towards Sustainable Cities,* Chapter 111, p.53.

2 See Henri Lefebvre (1968) *Le droit à la ville,* Paris, Edition Anthropos.

3 Peter Marcuse (2009), "From critical urban theory to the right to the city", in the *City,* Vol. 13, Nos. 2–3, June-September, p.185.

4 The National Union Party (l'Union national in French) was the conservative party of Québec, and was aligned with the doctrine of the Catholic Church and the conservative faction of the French-Canadian bourgeois elites.

5 For further study please see Donald Cuccioletta and Martin Lubin (2003), "The Québec Quiet Revolution: a Nosey Evolution?" in Michael D. Behiels and Matthew Hayday, Eds. In *Contemporary Québec,* McGill/Queen's University Press.

6 A good example of this can be understood in the play written by David Fenario, Balconville, where Francophone and Anglophone families shared a balcony and eventually understood that their struggle was not between English and French, but was a united working-class struggle in Point St. Charles. David Fenario is a radical activist author whose plays focused on the unity of the working class (French and English) against the capitalists.

7 See: "The New Urban Left: Parties Without Actors"

8 Please see, "Le Manifeste du FRAP", Noir et Rouge, 1969-1970, p.83-90, and the English translation in Annex 1.

9 IBID Annex 1 p.1

9 Please refer to Annex I, pages 1 and 2.

10 Please refer to Annex I, pages 3 and 4

11 In the Charter of the Caisse populaires, which were in every working-class neighborhood, the local Caisse poulaire had a social obligation to participate in the social problems of the neighborhood, if the board of directors voted so. Therefore, the strategy of taking over the administrative boards was directly linked to housing. Today we have examples of this with Batiment 7 in Point St Charles and in other working-class neighborhoods.

12 This is discussed further later in the paper.

13 Please see Annex I, p. 7-8

Further references

À Babord (1970), Revue sociale et politique, www.ababord.org, Élections à Montréal : La violence faite au FRAP.

Comby, Marc (2005), Mouvements sociaux, syndicates et action politique à Montréal, l'histoire du FRAP (1970–1974), memoire de maîtrise, décembre 2005, Université de Montréal

Comby, Marc, (2005), L'expérience du Front d'action politique des salaries (FRAP) à Montréal (1970–1974), Bulletin d'histoire politique (vol 9, #2) p.118-133.

Durand-Folco, Jonathan (2017), À Nous La Ville ; Traité de municipalisme, Écosociété.

Fortin, D. (1975), Le FRAP de Montréal, Memoire de maîtrise, Université Laval, pp 177

Front d'action politique : Les salaries au pouvoir! (1970), Montréal, Presses libres

Harvey, David (2012), Rebel Cities: From the Right to the City to the Urban Revolution, Verso Books

Harvey, David (2000), Spaces of Hope, University of California Press, Berkely, 2000.

Harvey, David, The Right to the City, International Journal of Urban and Regional Studies, 27(4), pp 939-994.

McGraw, Donald (1978), Le développement des groupes populaires à Montréal 1963-1973, Montréal, Éditions Saint-Martin

"Occupons la Ville," (2013), Nouveaux cahiers du Socialisme, #10, Fall

Roussopooulos, Dimitrios, (2017), The Rise of Cities : Montréal, Toronto, Vancouver and Other Cities, Black Rose Books

Saillant, François (2018), Lutter pour un toit : Douze batailles pour le logement au Québec, Écosociété

Wright, Erik Olin (2017) Utopies réelles, Paris, La Découverte

Dual Power and Taking the City beyond Elections

Bakur Rising:
Democratic Autonomy in Kurdistan

Nazan Üstündağ

*The Kurdish experiment in radical municipalism obliges us
to rethink the issue of state violence and how new worlds can
be created as well as defended.*

In recent years, following the collapse of the peace process between the Turkish state and the Kurdish freedom movement, the struggle for autonomy in the towns and cities of northern Kurdistan, or Bakur, has undergone a significant shift from a non-violent re-organization of social and political life to a militant self-defense movement.

The declaration of round-the-clock curfews in the summer of 2016 left many Kurdish cities under a *de facto* military siege, setting the scene for an urban war. Local youth dug trenches and built barricades to protect their neighborhoods and their democratic autonomous initiatives from police raids. While the guerrillas who had until then stayed up in the mountains came down to support the youth, Turkey's special forces tore apart towns and cities and razed entire neighborhoods to the ground. According to a UN report, at least 2,000 people died during these clashes.

The devastation of the war was not just material, however. The fact that Turkish special forces burnt civilians alive, stripped people naked, did not allow the bodies of those killed to be buried, and widely circulated images of mutilated dead bodies and cut-off limbs to celebrate their victory via social media, made a lasting mark on Kurdish people. Today, the experiment with democratic autonomy in urban Kurdistan has come to an end as thousands are imprisoned, organizations closed down, elected officials removed from office and towns and cities occupied by heavily armed security forces.

From Anti-Colonialism to Democratic Autonomy

The idea of democratic autonomy was developed in Kurdistan in the context of an armed struggle against Turkish occupation and colonization. In his book *The Wretched of the Earth*, Frantz Fanon argues that colonization is violence. The defining characteristic of a colonial regime is that its violence destroys nature, people and culture without ever needing to build consent. Many Western liberal legal regimes were formed within a framework of colonization. Such regimes protect the state's monopoly of violence against colonized communities as well as the right of the state to exert violence against its "others." By alluding to the imagined threat posed by the "other" to resort to violence to defend itself, liberal law transforms this possibility into an issue of security and thereby legitimizes and legalizes its own organized violence.

As the only internationally recognized discourse for the oppressed, claims of human rights violations are in turn burdened with the responsibility of producing evidence that the state has transgressed its legal and legitimate use of monopolized violence. Also, in order to sustain their legitimacy, human rights institutions are obliged to unquestionably condemn the violence used by actors other than the state and hence further contribute to the normalization of the state's monopoly on violence. Fanon invites those who struggle against colonization to create a world different from the one Western liberal law institutes.

Postcolonial writers who follow in Fanon's footsteps criticize the nation states that emerged after the anti-colonial struggles. They point out that nationalism has created a new hegemony in these states, shifting power from colonial elites to national elites and acting as a means by which colonized peoples enter the stage of global capitalism as workers and capitalists. In this process, peasants, women and the poor—who actively participated in the anti-colonial struggle—are sent back home, and the means to govern, produce, reproduce and defend themselves are confiscated from them by the newly independent state apparatus. They are then transformed into citizen-subjects capable of operating within and subjecting themselves to the social, economic and legal context shaped by a global capitalist reality.

In Kurdistan, the idea of democratic autonomy emerged as a response to this colonial and postcolonial experience. The Kurdish freedom movement can be understood as a movement that seeks to re-claim the means of self-governance, self-production, self-creation and self-defense from the Turkish state and the ruling elites of Kurdistan. Democratic autonomy invites people to transgress social relations and loyalties that have long been imposed on them. It promotes spaces where forms of representation and belonging can multiply to resist the homogenizing effect of the nation state, of the nuclear family, of capital and of positivist science.

Autonomy is not a turn inwards, nor does it denote independence from external relations. To the contrary: autonomy involves an engagement with multiple levels of conversation, negotiation and exchange. It suggests horizontality in place of the verticality instituted by the nation state and capital. Whereas capital seeks to secure geographies for accumulation, whereas the state system tries to homogenize social identities, and whereas the modern legal system attempts to monopolize the law and the legitimate use of force, democratic autonomy opens these up to a future of indeterminacy and possibility.

For the Kurdish freedom movement and its leader, Abdullah Öcalan, democratic autonomy is therefore a political form in which Kurds, Turks and other people in the Middle East can pursue empowerment and liberation and can struggle against nationalism, patriarchy and capitalism without recourse to the state-form. As such, the movement argues that the pursuit of democratic autonomy can serve as a means of peace-making in the wider region.

Autonomy and the Peace Process

Social scientists have long debated why post-conflict societies—from Ireland to South Africa—often face the disempowerment of emancipatory social forces. Some believe this to be a result of the fact that national regimes and peace processes have often been formulated by global capitalist actors whose primary goal is to secure capital accumulation, consolidate the nation state and invalidate ideologies alternative to neoliberalism.

Having learned from the negative experiences of the past, late-comers to the conflict resolution process like the PKK and the FARC therefore argue that the peace process should be seen as a social and political struggle more than a diplomatic endeavor—as a means rather than an end in itself. Society must exercise its self-defense and increase its capacity for freedom *during* the peace process. In other words, the spaces that open up during peace negotiations and peace struggles have to be seized upon as spaces for exercising freedom *here and now*. Only a society that can defend and govern itself can achieve peace without losing its potential for radical social transformation and its capacity to build alternative worlds.

This explains why the Kurdish freedom movement in Turkey has created various local, national and international institutions, brought various sections of the Kurdish and Turkish public together and formed new alliances during the peace process. It aimed to expand the space of negotiation by including new actors in the process through the many conferences it held and the three political parties it created. Meanwhile, Abdullah Öcalan, as the key negotiator of the Kurds, used the "negotiating table" as a platform to formulate a legal framework for the struggle for liberation.

The Turkish government, however, had other expectations of the peace process. It aimed at increasing its regional power by declaring itself as the representative of Kurds and Turks alike. Its objective was the disempowerment of the Kurdish freedom movement's discursive, representational and operational capacity. It hoped to secure Kurdish territories for the investment of capital, and to consolidate state power by promoting a collective Islamic identity that unite the varying historical trajectories of Kurds and Turks alike. In 2015, two years after it began, the Turkish government gave up the peace process and resorted once more to military means to deal with the "Kurdish question"—a decision that appears to have been motivated at least part by the fact that Kurdish groups were much more effective at using the peace process as a way to address various oppositional groups inside Turkey and bring them together against the policies of Erdogan's AKP government.

From Model to Movement

While Öcalan introduced the concept of democratic autonomy to the vocabulary and discourse of the Kurdish freedom movement in the early 2000s, it only became a subject of debate, criticism and elaboration for a wider public beyond the movement's cadres after the launching of a key meeting in Diyarbakır in 2010, when Kurdish activists invited Turkish journalists and intellectuals to evaluate their proposed solution to the Kurdish question. There, they presented their ideas of democratic autonomy and encountered a fierce opposition—not because the invited journalists and intellectuals were hostile to the recognition of Kurdish identity, but because they deemed this proposal to be utterly unrealistic.

Apart from a reform to the constitution that would exclude any reference to ethnicity, the proposal promoted by the Kurds had little to say about the restructuring of the Turkish state and the correcting of past wrongs. Rather, it included an elaborate model of self-governance and power-sharing where references like "people's parliaments," "communes," "peasants," and "women" expressed a desire to build a radical democracy in the political and economic realm as well as in health, education and other fields.

For the intellectuals of Turkey, who at the time were heavily invested in the fantasy of liberal democracy and the rule of law, the proposal seemed to be distracting energy and attention from "real issues." However, only a few years later, that which was once deemed unrealistic was already being practiced in many cities and towns across Kurdistan. Moreover, and somewhat ironically, the desires that informed the Gezi protests of 2013, when a million people took the streets of Istanbul and cities across Turkey, had an undeniable affinity with the demands for democratic autonomy as formulated by the Kurdish opposition.

Democratic autonomy in the Kurdish cities primarily involved the creation of assemblies at the local and regional level. Residential assemblies in neighborhoods, towns and cities would make decisions concerning infrastructure and other important social issues. In the local elections of 2009, the Kurdish opposition gained 97 municipalities and expanded this number to 99 in 2014. Now, however, these new municipal authorities had to respond to the demands of the unofficial people's assemblies, limiting their decision-making capacity and devolving the power of educated, middle-class elites and professionals to everyday people and workers. In addition to the general popular assemblies, there were also thematic assemblies on health, justice, the economy and education that aimed to democratize social policy and local governance.

While the economy assembly encouraged the formation of cooperatives and held meetings with businessmen, trade organizations and entrepreneurs along with the poor and the unemployed, the assemblies on public health provided free services and educated health workers. Academies opened up around Kurdistan providing ideological formation and skills training for those who participated in the construction of democratic autonomy, while truth and justice assemblies aimed to resolve local disputes to ensure that people in Kurdistan would stop using formal institutions of law and to promote the dissemination and democratization of community justice.

Another important characteristic of the democratic autonomy experiment in Kurdistan has been its strong feminist component. The Kurdish women's movement formed all-female assemblies in towns and cities and women held the right to veto decisions concerning women made in mixed-gender collectives. Furthermore, all assemblies and all formal institutions—including the municipality itself—had one woman and one man serving as co-presidents. In many mixed assemblies, the movement achieved the goal of equal representation of women and men.

Advances and Challenges

Between 2009 and 2015, different local, regional and national institutions and organizations—including assemblies, parties and congresses—continued to spread across Kurdistan. The Kurds already had extensive experience in building new models of self-governance as they had developed various organizations throughout the 1990s and 2000s to document human rights violations in the Kurdish regions—including forced displacements, disappearances and extra-judicial killings—and to assist villagers who had come to city centers as a result of the government's evacuation and destruction of their villages. The new forms of democratic autonomy built on these past experiences and were quickly put in place.

The strength of the experiment in democratic autonomy in Kurdistan came from dispute rather than harmony. Democracy was achieved by the fact that jurisdictions overlapped and sovereignties were being erased. It was precisely the social mobility and conflict between local actors generated by the creation of various assemblies, congresses, parties and institutions that caused more and more people to enter into local processes of decision-making and implementation. However, there were also some important problems with the construction and implementation of democratic autonomy in Bakur.

First of all, the model had been delineated in fairly detailed fashion beforehand, first by Öcalan and then by the PKK more generally, allowing it to become a means of social engineering. Second, the language of democratic autonomy was foreign to most people, and as such it produced movement elites who were experts in speaking this language at the expense of lay people on whom it imposed an alienating vocabulary. Third, autonomy was often interpreted as *national* autonomy and was understood to be the provision of services by the Kurdish movement rather than the state, without problematizing the wider relationship of "service provision" under capitalism, statism and patriarchy. Finally, certain sections of the population, especially the disadvantaged youth, could not be successfully incorporated into the institutions of democratic autonomy and remained isolated in their own organizations.

At the same time, however, this period was also one in which the Kurds further developed their repertoire of oppositional action. For one, the emergence of an autonomous government within the context of the war against ISIS in Rojava (northern Syria) influenced the struggle in Bakur immensely. In Rojava, the Kurdish freedom movement achieved universal recognition by means of armed struggle, and Kurdish youths learned and disseminated the tactics and strategies of urban warfare there.

Moreover, the peace process and the ceasefire between the Turkish army and the Kurdish forces allowed different people to visit and consult with the guerrillas at the PKK headquarters in the Qandil mountains of northern Iraq. Notably, the visibility and legitimacy that the freedom fighters acquired during the peace process firmly lodged the struggle in the imagination of ordinary Kurds. As opposed to the claustrophobia of urban spaces shaped by colonialism, capitalism and the patriarchal family, as well as the everyday conflicts that the formation of democratic autonomy inevitably entailed, guerrilla warfare represented an escape from family and work, an intimacy with nature, friendship and power. This was especially true for the urban youth. To the extent that they felt excluded from both formal political institutions and spaces of democratic autonomy, they popularized new practices within the cities that mimicked guerrilla warfare and transformed urban spaces into spaces of liberation here and now by means of armed resistance. Starting as self-defense units in neighborhoods fighting against the drug trade, prostitution and theft, these armed squads increasingly turned into urban guerrilla formations protecting neighborhoods from state violence.

Finally, people's relationship to rural areas underwent a major change during this time. Whereas in the previous period people's relationship with the rural areas had been uprooted by the experience of state violence and forced displacement, now urban actors slowly began to reattach themselves to the villages and the mountains. Children, women, men, party members and lay people, educated and non-educated, youngsters and elders walked along long roads into the countryside, resisting security forces and risking their lives together, engaging in multiple horizontal negotiations and conversations among themselves and with the guerrilla and security forces alike.

Urban Warfare

In the Kurdish cities, the youth and police often clash, with the former using stones and Molotov cocktails, and the latter rubber bullets, gas bombs and pressurized water. Already in 2013, however, these regular skirmishes had developed into more violent confrontations. While the guerrilla forces and the army maintained their ceasefire, a number of youth were shot during protests in the city. Moreover, those in urban areas also faced long prison sentences whenever the police caught them. Many of the youth were sons and daughters of the displaced, with little prospects in formal education and employment—contributing to an explosive social situation in the cities.

When ISIS attacked Kobani in 2014 and it began to look like the Turkish state was enabling the Kurdish city's siege, the youth took to the streets all over Bakur. That was the first time when the Turkish state realized the size and power of the Kurdish youth movement, and the fact that many of these youths were now lightly armed and well organized. After the defeat of ISIS at Kobani, the youth dug trenches in their neighborhoods to stop police raids aimed at arresting them. While the trenches were filled-up at Öcalan's request for de-escalation during the peace process, they were dug out again once the process collapsed.

Towards the end of 2015, Turkish special forces attacked these trenches with overwhelming force and a number of cities remained under siege for several months, while civilians were bombarded by tanks and targeted by snipers. Some of the guerrilla forces from the nearby mountains joined the youth in their campaign of self-defense. In late 2016, however, all rebelling cities were brought back under state control and reoccupied by state forces. Kurdish urban dwellers were able to survive the siege only because they shared food and safe spaces and had already established some basic autonomous health provision. Throughout 2017, in the wake of the failed coup attempt of the previous summer, the Turkish state engaged in a broad crackdown on all of its opponents, arresting Kurdish politicians, activists and youth. Many of the destroyed urban areas were confiscated by the state with the intention of rebuilding the cities in ways that would prevent any future insurgency.

The experiment with democratic autonomy in Kurdish cities and towns might seem like an extreme case in terms of the violence it unleashed from the state. Still, the Kurdish case poses some very important questions for those who want to imagine an alternative future to capitalism, the nation state and the patriarchal family. Although short-lived, the Kurds' experiment with democratic autonomy in Bakur, the various institutions they created and the negotiations they engaged in energized Turkey as a whole. On the other hand, because there was always already the external threat of the state, the internal problems that emerged in the process of self-governance remain undebated. Most importantly, the Kurdish case obliges us to rethink the issue of law and violence and how new worlds can be created as well as defended.

"Bakur Rising: Democratic Autonomy in Kurdistan" was originally published in Roar Magazine, Issue #6 (Summer 2017): 86-98.

Self-Reproduction and the Oaxaca Commune

Barucha Peller

The Oaxaca uprising of 2006 teaches us that any serious anti-capitalist movement must engage directly with the gendered logic of social reproduction.

In 2006 a popular mass uprising swept the southern state of Oaxaca, Mexico, galvanizing hundreds of thousands of participants around the region and removing state power from the capital city and dozens of other municipalities. For nearly six months, there were no police in Oaxaca City, and at one point the cityscape was transformed by up to 3,000 barricades.

After years of repressive, authoritarian rule at the hands of the Partido Revolucionario Institucional (PRI) and Governor Ulises Ruiz, the uprising was triggered by a violent eviction of a teachers' encampment in a central plaza during an annual strike of the Section 22 union on June 14. Thousands of Oaxacans poured into the streets to take back the square from police, and a spontaneous insurrection grew in which state authorities were physically removed and squares, government buildings, media outlets and city buses were taken over by protesters.

The movement formed a horizontal, central organizing body, the Popular Assembly of the People of Oaxaca (APPO), which demanded the ousting of Ulises Ruiz. For seven months one of the poorest states in Mexico attempted to reorganize society without state governance or capitalist social institutions. When broadcasts from occupied radio stations began to sign off with the slogan "Transmitting from the Oaxaca Commune," comparisons made to the historic Paris Commune were met with the response: "The Paris Commune lasted 70 days. We have lasted more than 100!"

The Oaxaca Commune ended on November 25, 2006 after the movement lost the battle for the streets to a violent and brutal siege by federal police and government-backed paramilitaries. By the end of the uprising, hundreds of people had been arrested and dozens were disappeared or assassinated.

Everyday Life at the Barricades

The formation of the Commune cannot be separated from the social organization of its everyday activity. The Oaxaca Commune was formulated not out of the means of the uprising—the barricades, the occupations—but out of the social relations formed by organizing everyday life to reproduce such means. Rather than being atomized into the home, the reproduction of everyday life was reorganized to disavow the capitalist logic of a gendered social division of labor and to give way to communal resourcing, belonging and life as a terrain of struggle.

While the APPO provided a formal alternative to state governance as a political body, the incredible longevity of the Oaxaca uprising and the takeover of the capital by the movement meant that questions of everyday life and the informal economy became key sites of contestation and a project of the political imagination in their own right. During the uprising the women's movement directly raised some of these questions and also demonstrated that a conscious confrontation with the social division of labor is necessary to build a commune that actually challenges state power through the de-commodification of common resources and the de-privatization of domestic and reproductive labor.

A central contradiction in the Oaxaca Commune, as we will see, was therefore based around the social, political and strategic questions that arose when men attempted to uphold the gendered division of labor and force women back into the home.

The barricades that made up the cityscape of the Oaxaca Commune were not only sites of physical defense against military attacks, but were also home to a myriad of reproductive activities in which historically feminized labor became the basis for transformed social relations. The barricades were places where the people of Oaxaca slept, cooked and shared food, had sex, shared news, and came together at the end of the day. Resources such as food, water, gasoline and medical supplies were re-appropriated and redistributed, and in the same way, reproductive labor was re-appropriated from the specialized sphere of the home and became the underscoring way to reimagine social life and collective bonds.

Rather than returning home at night and turning on the television, Oaxacans would return to the barricades and listen to transmissions from occupied radio stations together before turning in for the night on makeshift beds of cardboard and blankets. At all hours of the day, coffee was carried out of homes or businesses and was brewed over fires at the barricade and passed around. Romantic messages and "shout-outs" were sent between participants on different barricades via the occupied radio.

Everyday events at the barricades, from distributing food from a Doritos truck that had been re-appropriated after being stopped on the highway to holding educational workshops, recreated a community infrastructure that is usually naturalized as women's labor in the home and in neighborhoods. People belonged to the Commune simply because they took part in this reproduction of daily life—from cooking at the barricades, carrying coffee to the barricades from homes or businesses, carrying news between barricades, to making molotovs at barricades, stacking rocks or simply sharing stories.

Maintaining the barricades through maintaining day-to-day life on the barricades excavated the "home" and the work women do in the home as a buried site of isolated, unrecognized labor to reformulate such activities as public and collective relationships of struggle. The social organization of reproductive labor on the barricades began to erode the capitalist, gendered division of labor in which reproductive labor creates value or labor capacity elsewhere for capitalist extraction. The collectivization and generalization of reproductive activities allowed the movement to become increasingly "self-reproducing" and as such increasingly threatening to the social order.

Self-reproduction, or the movement's ability to directly reproduce itself in day-to-day terms without the mediation of a gendered division of labor or an invisibilized labor force of women doing all the tasks necessary to maintain life so that the movement could persist, meant that the Oaxaca uprising reproduced itself as Commune. Self-reproduction forged a collective subjectivity out of the barricades as a shared experience of everyday life.

When people began to identify themselves as *barricadistas*, and then by specific barricades ("I am from la Barricada de Cinco Changos," or "I am from la Barricada de Sonora"), there was a clear shift in subjective identification away from roles assigned by waged labor ("I am a doctor" or "I am a student") or other subjectivities organized by capitalism. In these ways, the Commune forged subjects that identified not by the commodification of their labor but by the collectivization of everyday relationships and the means of self-reproduction at the barricades.

Given this need for the Commune to arise out of self-reproduction, it is not surprising that it was common to find mostly women at the barricades, or that many barricades were all women. Women found that the terrain of struggle was precisely in the informal relationships required to hold communities together. Barricades also tended to protect the primary battlegrounds where the Commune was being forged, in neighborhoods and media occupations.

As the months of the uprising carried on and the numbers of assassinated and disappeared mounted, women participated in the protection of the barricades through nightly patrols and defenses against las caravanas de la muerte, the pickup trucks of paramilitaries who frequently shot up the barricades. Women began to assume the type of revolutionary political activities that have historically been defined as masculine.

The Women's Television Occupation

The flashpoint of the Oaxaca Commune, and what was understood as the emergence of a women's movement, was the bold takeover of the state television and radio station, Canal Nueve, by thousands of women on August 1, 2006. Enraged at the media for spreading lies about the movement, an all-women's march called the cazerola (pots and pans) converged on the doors of the station and demanded 15 minutes of airtime. When they were denied, women forced their way into the station and spontaneously took it over. The women quickly taught themselves how to use the station's equipment and began statewide television and radio broadcasts.

Although by August the APPO had been broadcasting from two radio stations in the capital city, the horizon of possibilities for the movement broadened beyond what anyone had imagined when the high-powered transmissions of the state television and radio stations were in the hands of the women of the Oaxaca uprising. Collectivizing communication and creating media as a communal form was a necessary part of reclaiming everyday life in terms of what these women called its "truths." Many women who took over the station referred repeatedly to presenting the "truth" as a motivation for taking over the station and, as one woman aptly put it, "to present a little bit of so much truth that exists."

This "so much truth" that the women sought to unveil on the radio and television station was a description of the economic and social conditions experienced by the communities most vulnerable to the socially destructive effects of neoliberal structural adjustment and the racist and repressive hegemony of the PRI. The privatization of public resources not only has deep neo-colonial effects on indigenous groups, which make up 70 percent of the population of Oaxaca state, but capitalist enclosures of resources and services such as education, healthcare and basic community infrastructure burdened women particularly, as such issues tend to be heavily "feminized" and mystified as "women's work."

The women's broadcasts thus brought together indigenous groups, the urban poor and housewives to analyze these everyday realities across the state and to galvanize people to participate in the uprising. The ability of the "masses" to communicate en masse revealed not only a collective suffering but a collective will to continue en la lucha. The Commune may not have known itself as such were it not for the images and voices of so many others and the collective truths that were transmitted from the occupied station.

Gendered Contradiction

The tension over upholding the gendered, social division of labor became a central limit to the Oaxaca Commune realizing a collective identity in struggle. This contradiction arose in the Canal Nueve occupation and persisted on the barricades. When women fought to take control of social reproduction at the barricades and on the plantones (the occupied squares) by refusing to limit their contributions to the movement to the private sphere, domestic violence and threats as well as men's refusal to collectivize work in the home undermined the entire structure of Commune and women's ability to remain in the streets. As Ita, a participant in the Canal Nueve takeover explained:

There were comrades who complained that since August 1 (the takeover of Canal Nueve) their partner was absent. There were many women who suffered domestic violence for being at the occupations and marches, sometimes their husbands even attempted to divorce or separate. The husbands didn't take well to the idea of women abandoning the housework to participate politically. They didn't help in the sense of doing the housework, such as taking care of kids or washing clothes, so that the women could continue being at the station.

The number of women circulating at the Canal Nueve occupation dwindled little by little as women had no other choice but to return home and take care of children or perform other domestic labor. On August 21, after three weeks of the Canal Nueve occupation, paramilitaries took advantage of the low numbers and shot up the network transmitters, rendering them useless. And yet the women were relentless: they came into the streets again the next day and led movement participants to take over and occupy ten different radio stations, four of which remained in the hands of the Commune for an extended period.

While housework required many women to return home, women on the whole did not solemnly submit to patriarchal violence and threats. One woman continued to defend a barricade after her husband broke her arm to prevent her from going to the streets. As Eva, a housewife, noted: "Nobody came to take us out of our houses saying, 'go to the struggle'. On the contrary, they said: 'stop leaving the house, calm down'—they repressed us. But we dared."

So conscious were women of the gendered contradictions that were sure to arise due to their participation in the uprising that they hung a banner in the occupied television studio that appeared on screen during the first broadcasts reading: "When a woman moves forward, not one man is left behind." In this respect, women tried to appeal to a sense of class belonging, suggesting that the women's movement was an advancement for the class as a whole. Nevertheless, the tension over women's participation in the movement was never resolved for the greater strategic or political project of the Commune. As Eva put it simply: "we kept fighting on two different fronts—against the system, and with the men inside our own movement."

Reproductive labor was at once a limit to women's participation as well as a galvanizing force for women's autonomy and collective organizing. The power of communication and sociability in identifying and forging collective struggles did not only occur in the occupied media broadcasts but also in the informal discussions between women in the Canal Nueve occupation. When for the first times in their lives women had a space autonomous from men, they found that the authoritarian regime of the state and the economy extended into their experience of the social division of labor and everyday life in the home and with family. As Ita put it: "The beautiful thing that happened there was that at night all of us women began to talk about our life stories, and that's where we got more rage to continue in this struggle—not just to topple the government, but to organize as women to confront what the majority of us are living."

Being part of the Commune therefore did not mean that women universalized their political participation alongside everyone else, but that they understood their participation as specified by their struggle against the social division of labor and capitalism's commodification of reproductive labor inside the home. The tension over upholding the social division of labor meant that for women fighting the government and fighting over reproductive labor became one and the same struggle.

Revolutionizing everyday life by taking back spaces and resources from their commodified and privatized forms was a central tenet of the Oaxaca Commune. It underpinned the way in which the movement evolved from its central demand to remove the governor to an articulation of how his policies had upheld capitalism's encroachment on every sphere of public life. But it was the women's articulation of exploitation in the home that truly called for a reorganization of everyday life outside of the logic of capitalism.

Informal Processes of Collectivization

Just as reproductive and unwaged labor is often informal, the informal social relations and the daily gestures of solidarity and mutual aid within the Commune constituted a political imaginary beyond—and at times without—the formal representations of the movement, the APPO.

In analyzing the Oaxaca uprising, the left has mostly centralized the APPO in its attempts to describe and account for the incredible seven months of insurrection against capitalism and the state. But this focus on purely formal organizing structures of the movement mimics in a sense the capitalist division of labor, in which value is only produced in a formal sphere, overlooking the social aspects of organizing that occurred beside public political demands and organizations. While the APPO was described as a movement of movements, and the political demands issued from the APPO—mainly the removal of the governing party—encompassed a collective political will, its description did not serve to encompass the informal processes of collectivization that struggled with the question of reproducing everyday life.

The sense of collective identity that underscored the Oaxaca Commune was not solely an identification with the APPO. In fact, many participants—especially housewives and the urban poor—identified themselves as militants of the uprising but not as a part of the APPO. It would require an entire separate sociological inquiry to examine all the reasons why participants in the uprising did not identify with the APPO or how the APPO failed to encompass the whole of the demographically diverse sectors of the uprising in its particular structures of organization and representation; certainly, women fought unsuccessfully for more equalized participation in the APPO, giving rise to another gendered contradiction of the uprising. It was not until November, seven months after the uprising began, that the APPO brought gender representation into express consideration, and failed then, even after the momentous women's movement, to account for participatory parity.

Ultimately, the experience of everyday life that formulated the Oaxaca Commune and the articulations of women participants concerning the limitations of the Commune help broaden our understanding of struggle as a confrontation with ways in which capitalism has commodified reproductive labor into a feminized sphere—in which any serious anti-capitalist movement must engage directly with the gendered logic of the reproduction of collective social life.

"Self-Reproduction and the Oaxaca Commune" was originally published in Roar Magazine, Issue #1 (Spring 2016): 70-78.

Beyond Projet Montréal: Progressive Environmentalism and the Challenges of Real Existing Municipalism

Jonathan Durand-Folco

In November 2017, the green municipal party Projet Montréal (PM) made waves by winning a majority of City Council seats. Despite the majority of polls and columnists predicting that the incumbent mayor Denis Coderre would easily win the local elections, PM's Valérie Plante became the first female mayor in the history of Montréal. With her election, many had high expectations for PM—the first progressive municipal administration since the Montréal Citizens Movement that governed the city from 1986–1994—with their center-left program that covered issues related to mobility, economic development, sustainability, social justice, participatory democracy, and more. How do we move beyond these expectations to critically assess the achievements, failures, and blind spots of the first half of the Plante administration's term? In order to make a rigorous appraisal of the situation, we will briefly present Projet Montréal's political framework or ideology as a political party and identify some internal tensions that occurred in the history of the organization. We will then summarize the main achievements and major problems of the first two years of the Plante administration, as well as identify some factors that may explain the options and constraints PM has faced since they took office. Finally, we will explore potential avenues for further action and reflect on the challenges of "real existing municipalism."

A Brief Portrait of Projet Montréal

Projet Montréal was founded by Richard Bergeron and a group of urban planners, environmental activists, and citizens in May 2004. Centered on the promotion of urban sustainability, with human-scale neighborhoods, streets designed for bikes and pedestrians, green spaces, and intelligent planning, Projet Montréal was initially conceived and perceived as a broad environmentalist coalition. Over time, it attracted people that were affiliated with several parties at provincial and federal levels like the New Democratic Party, Liberals, Parti Québécois, and Québec Solidaire.

Since municipal politics in Québec and Canada are not usually thought of within the left-right divide, or on the sovereigntist-federalist spectrum, PM attracted a variety of people from several progressive and centrist ideologies. They were united around a common project to reduce car traffic, improve residents' quality of life, reverse urban sprawl, increase affordable housing, promote citizen participation, and social innovations. Since its foundation, PM has never been a truly left-wing or radical ecologist party based on a social transformation perspective; rather it has been a pragmatic, social-democratic (or social-liberal) environmentalist organization searching to improve the city through sustainable development.

That being said, PM has sometimes been publicly perceived as a "radical" formation, especially under the leadership of Luc Ferrandez, the mayor of the Plateau-Mont-Royal borough. Since he was elected in the 2009 local elections, he adopted strong measures like inverting street directions, banning advertising panels, planting thousands of trees, etc. Despite criticism from many local business owners, right-wing columnists and some citizens, he was re-elected twice in 2013 with 51.3%, and in 2017 with 65.7% of the votes. Ferrandez rapidly became the most well-known figure of PM, appearing as a radical, yet pragmatic and charismatic, politician willing to confront the establishment in the interest of the public.

In November 2014, the founder and leader of the party Richard Bergeron suddenly left PM to join Denis Coderre's executive committee, in order to oversee urban development projects like the covering of the Ville-Marie Expressway and a new potential tram system. Luc Ferrandez became the interim leader, but due to fears that he was perceived as too "controversial" or "radical" by the public, he refused to be the permanent leader of the party. Projet Montréal held its first leadership race in Fall 2016. This process revealed ideological oppositions inside the organization.

On one side, Guillaume Lavoie presented himself as a progressive, centrist figure, advocating for the (de)regulation of the "sharing economy" (including Uber and Airbnb) using a "modern" and technocratic approach of urban administration. Lavoie personified the young, professional, "Third Way" politician (like Justin Trudeau or Emanuel Macron), or what Nancy Fraser would call a "progressive neoliberal," combining entrepreneurial values with a focus on sustainable mobility and inclusion. On the other side, Valérie Plante entered the leadership race as a feminist, Left-wing figure from the social sector, with a program focused on the $15 minimum wage, the expansion of the Montréal metro system with the "Pink Line," affordable housing, etc.

At first, Guillaume Lavoie had the support from the "establishment" of the party (a great majority of municipal councillors from PM) and many public figures (mostly centrists and neoliberals). As such, he felt he could easily win the race. But Valérie Plante succeeded in mobilizing people from the Left (mostly from the NDP and Québec Solidaire) with a "rank and file" campaign, finally winning the leadership race with 51.9% of the votes. Though this close result did split the party, it did reveal the important need to "reweld" the party before the municipal elections.

While the political platform of PM included many progressivist measures (participatory budgeting, $15 minimum wage, major investments in social housing), the electoral strategy for the 2017 campaign presented Valérie Plante as *l'homme de la situation* (the man for the job) against Denis Coderre, and relied on a catch-all discourse with car traffic reduction, low taxes, and the Pink Line. In the end, the pitting of the setbacks of the incumbent mayor (with the Formula E scandal and a relatively boring campaign) against Valérie Plante's dynamic, original, and enthusiastic campaign earned her victory at the municipal elections. PM won with a comfortable majority in city hall, with 11 borough mayors and 34 councillors.

Reality check: Accomplishments and Concessions of a New Administration

Projet Montréal's first accomplishment was the election of a young, unknown, woman with a progressive sensibility to the head of the city, defeating a well-established and confident career politician. As Marx wrote about the Paris Commune, its first social measure "was its own working existence." In the first days in office, Plante adopted several measures to distance herself from the Coderre administration. First, she cancelled the three-year contract with the Formula E in response to the financial fiasco—though this move resulted in a $33 million lawsuit against her and the city. She also cancelled the anti-pitbull bill and announced major investments in public transportation with the announcement of 300 new electric buses.

Two months after taking office, Plante made her first "political mistake" with a controversial tax-hike. Even though it was a relatively small increase, Plante had promised during the campaign that she would deliver on all her promises without raising taxes. At first, she evaded criticism by blaming the previous administration for over-spending and, at first, managed to brush aside criticism from the opposition and angry citizens. Ultimately however, when Plante faced her first public backlash, she admitted to having made a mistake and promised not to raise taxes in her coming years in office.

Despite this first misstep, the greatest achievements of the Plante administration so far are related to mobility issues. She convinced the provincial and federal governments to fund the extension of the Blue Line (after more than thirty years of failed attempts!) and has already secured support for the first part of the Pink Line, a tramway connecting downtown and the neighborhood of Lachine. She also announced the launch of a Bicycle Express Network, adopted strict bylaws for privately-owned Jump bikes and Lime scooters, and reduced restrictions on car-share services (Car2go and Communauto). By the end of her first term, Plante will probably become the most important "mobility mayor" in Montréal history.

Other important social measures that she championed include the creation of the Montréal Food Policy Council, public meetings with the police for greater accountability, participatory budgeting in Hochelaga-Maisonneuve and Ahuntsic-Cartierville boroughs, free transit for 160,000 young low income people, and a new 20-20-20 strategy to force developers to set aside 20% of new housing units for social housing, 20% for affordable housing, and 20% for family-size units. The Montréal Gazette tracked 18 promises Valérie Plante made for the first year in office and she has already realized 16 of them.

Plante initially took a strong stance against the conservative provincial government's proposed Bill 21, which would ban government employees from wearing religious symbols, but she yielded, announcing that the city will enforce the provisions of Bill 21 once approved. This kind of compromise is not an exception, but a common feature of the Plante administration. For example, she abandoned the label of "sanctuary city," preferring to talk of a "responsible and engaged city," which is more inclusive and offers more job opportunities and protection for migrants. Furthermore, the 20-20-20 strategy is less radical than it first appears, due to the fact that developers can bypass the rule if they pay the city compensation in land or cash. While she was strongly opposed to the Royalmount megamall project in 2017, Plante declared that, while Montréal cannot support the project, "the city is powerless to delay construction." Is the Plante administration really constrained by higher forces, is it making regular use of "cost-benefit calculations," or using a triangulation strategy to overcome the divide between social and economic actors?

Our claim is that Projet Montréal's administration is effectively restrained by economic, political, and legal constraints that limit the possibility of social change, but that it simultaneously adopts a pragmatic-centric stance, especially towards economic issues. For example, Plante appealed to the financial sector in her victory speech by mentioning that "Montréal is open for business." This declaration doesn't seem to be only a tactic to reassure the economic elite that supported Denis Coderre, but a genuine approval of the dominant economic model. It is no surprise then that their 2018-2022 economic development strategy focuses on "high-potential sectors" (like cultural and creative industries, life sciences and health technologies, digital industry, mobility and transport, and cleantech sector), and includes eight action plans for entrepreneurship, optimization of business services, knowledge and talent, international economic affairs, social innovation, commerce, economic development of the territory, and design.

Plante also mentioned that she was disappointed that Montréal didn't make the shortlist for Amazon headquarters, and delivered an enthusiastic speech when artificial intelligence multinational corporations decided to expand in Montréal. Therefore, the economic program of PM is not centered on social economy or alternative economic models, but reproduces the dominant model of globalized digital capitalism, combined with an entrepreneurial version of social innovation taking the form of hubs for start-ups in vacant and public buildings. If Plante created a rupture with the Coderre Administration on social and environmental issues, she uncritically embraces the same model of economic development based on the "creative class," in continuity with Guillaume Lavoie's "progressive neoliberalism."

In other words, PM remains progressive on social justice issues, but doesn't propose a genuine change in urban economic development. Plante's administration doesn't have any plans to seriously tackle real-estate speculation, and the measures taken to improve residents' quality of life often contribute to eco-gentrification. In the summer of 2019, Plante refused to acknowledge that Montréal has a housing crisis, and instead invested public money to improve and expand middle class access to private home ownership, therefore reinforcing the speculation dynamic that makes cities like Vancouver and Toronto so expensive.

Ecological Crisis and the Challenges of "Real Existing Municipalism"

The contradiction between the social and economic dimensions of PM goes along with a tension on the "environmental question" that evokes the historical debate between the *fundis* (radicals) and the *realos* (realists) in green parties. In May 2019, Luc Ferrandez unexpectedly announced he was leaving politics, because he no longer wanted to "fool citizens into believing that we are collectively making every effort to slow down the rate of destruction of our planet." Within the Plante administration, he was responsible for large parks and green spaces on the executive committee, and despite many environmental measures (on fossil-fuel investments, one-time-use plastic bags, engagement for a carbon neutral city in 2050), he believed the city of Montréal wasn't doing enough to struggle against climate change. "What I am proposing is nothing short of a war effort. It is only out of indulgence towards our worst faults that we refuse to see that an extinction is worth a war and that victory is worth the sacrifice of a few hundred thousand votes," Ferrandez said.

This sudden decision wasn't meant as a global dismissal of Plante leadership or of Projet Montréal overall orientation, but as a wake-up call for a radical shift in the context of the climate emergency. Nicolas Hulot, the former minister of ecological transition under the Macron government, made a similar move in April 2018; he resigned because he felt that "tiny steps" were largely insufficient to tackle environmental challenges, especially when taking the "presence of lobbyists in circles of power" into account. During the springtime flooding that affected many people in Montréal and cities across Québec in 2019, Ferrandez published a Facebook post titled "Fuck you, all of us," where he criticized passionately our collective immobilism toward climate change. He wanted the city to adopt strong measures such as buying up green space in the city and turning all non-residential parking spots into paid spots, but the members of Plante's executive committee thought that this would spark a huge public backlash. The ghost of the 2018 tax hike made the PM administration afraid of radical "unpopular" measures and the cabinet was already preoccupied with the next elections.

What Can We Learn from This Experience?

First, a progressive local government must learn to overcome the fear of backlash related to "unpopular decisions," be that for social justice, ecological transition, or alternative economic development schemes. If "real life politics" inevitably involves making compromises every once in a while, "radical measures" for the general interest can also be advantageous during elections. Ferrandez has shown this twice with each of his re-elections in the face of strong, adverse, reactions from a large opposition in the borough and the media.

Second, an environmentalist local government should take the opportunity of a flood crisis and a "state of emergency" to adopt stronger measures that foster urban resilience and fight climate change. Even if Projet Montréal adopts an urban sustainability approach rather than an "ecosocialist" framework, it would still be possible to make "radical decisions" that would concretely build a different future and contribute to social transformation. In other words, the most important thing in "urban politics" is not so much your ideology, but the attitude, courage, and actions you implement when faced with complexity and adversity. In this regard, even if Ferrandez does not identify as a "Left-wing activist," and does not care much about social justice issues or participatory democracy, he is more "radical" or "revolutionary" than Valérie Plante, especially on the ecological question.

Third, even if it is essential to tackle social and environmental issues at the municipal level, it is also necessary to articulate those measures with a critical and realistic analysis of the dynamics of global capitalism and the private interests of economic elites. The separation of the social and economic dimensions of public action is probably the distinctive feature separating "progressive urban management" or "social-democratic municipalism," from the "radical municipalism" embodied by Spain's Rebel Cities like Barcelona and Madrid. Instead of promoting traditional economic growth on the one hand (which reinforces social inequalities, real estate speculation and gentrification), and implementing "inclusion policies" on the other hand, it would be rather useful to regulate and raise taxes for big corporations and capitalist digital platforms (like Airbnb), while orienting local economic development model towards notions of solidarity economy, urban commons, (re)municipalization of public services and land, etc.

Fourth, another difference between a progressive environmental party like Projet Montréal and a citizen's platform like Barcelona en Comú lies in the simultaneous involvement of social movements inside and outside the institutions. Even if PM does represent a real political party with a democratic life and militant activists, it wasn't born as a coalition of social movements seeking to "occupy the institutions" and transform the city. Yet, several citizen groups across the city (like Action-Gardien in the Pointe-Saint-Charles neighborhood, the Comité d'action de Parc-Extension, the Milton Parc Community, À nous les quartiers, and the Montréal Urban Left), gather a number of activists who organize collective actions and public conferences that slowly try to influence the Plante administration. A healthy municipalist movement implies not only a progressive local government, but strong social movements and citizen actions that try to build a form of dual power.

Is There a "Real Existing Municipalist Movement" in Montréal?

If we consider the new political context ushered in by the victory of Projet Montréal and the first important measures adopted by the Plante administration, in addition to the presence of urban struggles against gentrification in several neighborhoods, and the emergence of a radical municipalist consciousness in some grassroots organizations, there seems to be a real, but nascent, municipalist movement in Montréal.

Once again, the will for social transformation cannot simply be measured by the level of "radicality" of a party's ideology, or the discourse a mayor holds in a particular political, cultural, and historical context. Real existing municipalism is about the concrete measures that a "fearless city" adopts to defend social rights, promote solidarity economy, municipalize land and public services, support urban commons, and put in place the building blocks of a new ecological and democratic society. A municipal government cannot institute radical policies without massive support from civil society and/or the contestation from social movements that keep the pressure on elected representatives.

In that sense, even if Projet Montréal wasn't created as a radical leftist party seeking to overthrow globalized neoliberal capitalism, it opens a window of opportunity for social movements and citizen groups who want to experiment with new forms of direct democracy, social innovations, mutual aid, community economic development, and socio-ecological resilience.

An Interview with Kali Akuno

Jonny Gordon-Farleigh

Jonny Gordon-Farleigh (JGF): Cooperation Jackson is part of a patient political project building an alternative economy for the city's black-majority residents and the 'Eastern black belt portions' of Mississippi. Could you explain the historical background to the Jackson-Kush Plan and how it inspired the launch of Cooperation Jackson?

Kali Akuno (KA): I think it's important to acknowledge there were many streams that led to Cooperation Jackson. It's also important to have a real understanding of how it long it takes, in many respects, to build a base and organize for something to emerge and grow. One of the oldest foundations of the Jackson-Kush plan, which is strategy underlining the operations Cooperation Jackson, was the birth of the Provisional Government of the Republic of New Afrika (PG-RNA)—nearly 51 years ago now. The PG-RNA was launched in Detroit in March 1968, and it came out of the Black Power movement era and was devised to be a means to realize self-determination for Black people. Black people in the United States were being confronted and out of this struggle was a declaration of independence that lay the foundation for the provisional government. This was followed by a concrete move in 1971 where key organizers and activists looked to make a small town outside of Jackson, Mississippi, the capital of the provisional government. Many people moved here in the same year and opened a space that was immediately attacked by the US Federal Government.

I talk about this experience because it was the beginning of the work to organise the West Jackson community. It's not an accident that the concentration of Cooperation Jackson's work is in the Poindexter neighbourhood, the place of the original provisional government house and where the deepest level of organising has happened since 1971.

Today we represent a younger generation that are coming to build on the foundation in this neighbourhood, and we are a core of people who share the politics, are familiar with the history, and have been part of some of the sacrifices over the years.

We are an extension of this movement that is organising in the Kush District—18 contiguous black-majority counties that span both sides of the lower Mississippi river, starting in Memphis, Tennessee to New Orleans, Louisiana. The overwhelming concentration of this district is in the Mississippi Delta, an area that is larger than Belgium. Within this region there is the legacy of chattel slavery, in particular, the heavy concentration of the production of cotton and sugar. This is, of course, why there was and still is a heavy concentration of communities of African descent.

It is also where a quarter of all elected officials in the United States originate, so it's not an insignificant region and the basis of why people came to this region and understood its importance. This is also why it has been considered a launching pad, a place to amass political power to help improve the overall quality of life and create more liberty for those of African descent.

To personalise this history, one of the young people who decided to take up the challenge to move to Mississippi was Chokwe Lumumba, shortly after finishing his undergraduate degree. Of course, 40-odd years later he becomes a city councillor and then becomes the elected mayor of Jackson. This was part of a 50-year project that started in 1971, and the Jackson-Kush plan was built on this run of success over the last decade.

JGF: In the Jackson-Kush plan you outline the intention to build 'dual power', primarily through people's assemblies, but also though 'engaging electoral politics on a limited scale'. Could you explain this reluctant relationship with electoral politics?

KA: In the United States, our electoral system is winner-takes-all, there is no proportional representation. If a candidate wins one more vote than the next candidate, they assume office for two or four years, depending on term limits. The newly elected official then crafts and implements policies based on their views and opinions. That's one dimension of our political situation. Then there's one difference with the UK. In the UK, the Conversative and the Labour parties represent platforms, views, and traditions, and for the most part, as I understand it, UK voters are not only voting for the individual but a broader programme of policies. At the same time, UK politicians have to adhere to these policies and views to retain their seats and cabinet positions. The United States is profoundly different—the Democratic and Republican parties do not really operate as platforms. In this country you are voting for an individual as there is nothing that binds an individual politician to follow the party platform or adhere to the party's principles or strategies. It is really up to individual discretion. There are few mechanisms—apart from voting a politician in or out—that hold politicians accountable. In the US you are reliant on the vote, financial pressure, or flooding a campaign with election resources. Or, if you have to go another route, you can organise as many people as you possibly can to exert political impact through direct action. This is critical to the understanding of the Jackson-Kush plan within the US political system, and why we have a cautious relationship with electoral politics.

Within the context of electing politicians into government, the dominant orientation of our political system at the moment is neoliberalism. Cooperation Jackson are consciously and intentionally trying to counter this through building institutions, such as people's assemblies. More importantly, though, we are trying to do things that governments, under neoliberalism and austerity, will not do or lack the resources to execute.

We start with the notion that no-one is coming to save us and if we adopt this orientation—if there are critical things we want to happen—we need to make them happen with the resources at our immediate disposal. This notion of creating dual power rests on this approach. One side is holding the government accountable to the social contract, then on the other side we are actively improving our lives through self-organisation. Those are the real questions that dual power seeks to answer. These efforts, in our case, to ask a state government that is dominated by white supremacists, is a road to nowhere. We have to build our capacity and strength and execute what we want. So basically we do not ignore electoral politics but it cannot and will not meet all our needs and realise our desires. So the challenge of the dual approach, for us, is standing up for ourselves as we see fit. To get thousands of people to agree on anything is not an easy task. Our community does not have a lot of wealth or wherewithal, but there is a huge amount of talent.

JGF: You were in the political administration of Chokwe Lumumba, supporting the election of the first Black mayor in Jackson, Mississippi in 2013. Black-led electoral strategies have heritage in US politics—especially in the 1970s and 80s. How do you reflect on your recent experience?

KA: It's a mixed bag at best. One thing I had been warning about when we assumed mayoral office in 2013 was that the local economy was much stronger than in previous years. At that time the city had financial reserves for various infrastructure repair projects, to support municipal pay raises, and it was possible to use a standard business model approach to give more purchasing power and stimulate demand. In 2016/7 the economy was in a different place and state-led political forces really lined up against the city as retribution for the election of a black mayor.

From 2016 there was a very clear and concerted effort by the Republican Party—essentially the Tea Party—to eat away at Jackson's economic base and erode the autonomy of the municipality. The first major move was for the state government to control Jackson *Medgar Wiley Evers International Airport,* aiming to take advantage of a strip mall development opportunity, generating more tax revenue and redirecting profits to the state government. This measure would not take the property away from the city, as it owned it, but remove administrative control and direction of profits. The proposal was put through the state legislature and it passed, giving control of these assets to the State Governor. For context, the current Mississippi State Governor is Field Bryant, the nephew of the woman who accused Emmett Till of whistling at her, which led to the 14-year old's lynching in 1955. It was her uncle, also Field Bryant's uncle, who was part of the lynch mob that executed Emmett Till. This is our Governor and his family heritage.

To go back to this particular measure, it was used to strip the city of any control of these assets. This is important because most of our economy is structured around two things. Firstly, it's the state capital of Mississippi, so the largest employer in town are the federal, state, county, and municipal governments. Secondly, for the transnational economy, it's an important transport hub, with air freight and railroad infrastructure distributing products North, East, South, and West. The city of Jackson sits in a strategic crossroads with the 55 freeway as a trade corridor, connecting New Orleans through Jackson to Chicago. We are also on the T crossroads on the i-20 between metropolitan Atlanta and metropolitan Dallas-Fort Worth. So as a transport node, if the city loses control of these assets, the economic impact is clear.

There were other things. We knew there was a major play to privatize our education system, and the city was put under an Environmental Protection Agency mandate, obligating major repairs to our water system. We knew that the city did not have the resources for the infrastructural overhaul, and that it was part of a major drive towards a regionalisation or privatisation of our water system. And we knew, during mayoral campaigns for the last election, that we did not have a clear enough strategy or resources. I started calling the situation a 'Syriza Trap': if we assumed the mayor's office with an obligation to manage the city's affairs, we were putting ourselves in a position to administer austerity and privatisation. Myself and others wanted to avoid this situation, especially after witnessing what happened in Greece.

In 2017 the newly elected mayor was Chokwe Antar Lumumba, the son of Chokwe Lumumba, someone who broadly agreed with the Jackson- Kush plan. As part of his new role, Lumumba experienced the Governor's first major play on his watch—the privatisation of the school district. Even though it is now state controlled, the Governor has left the local apparatus intact. So right now we're living through this experiment with our public system, where I have two children, and where the government can change its mind and not be accountable to anyone. We do not have local governance, only local administration.

So it's definitely a mixed bag. We have a mayor who shares our worldview and politics, but whose hands are tied. We are in a situation of constantly trying to push the Jackson-Kush plan to the best of their ability, and block the government and big business. The city administration are, really, caught between a rock and a hard place, and our movement, to a certain extent, is also caught here, too. Now it's about how we figure out, under these new terms and conditions, how do we realize our programme.

JGF: The 'new' or 'radical' municipalism is a term to describe the use of electoral politics by social movements in towns, cities, or city-regions. How do you understand the relationship and tensions between local, national, and international politics?

KA: For us, there is a long-term view that goes beyond the short-term crisis of austerity I've just described. We have to make international links to really counter the impositions of new technologies and global institutions and businesses, such as Airbnb and Uber. These businesses are changing the economy, who it serves and who orchestrates it. For us, similar to many world cities, thousands of people are being pushed out of their neighbourhoods as homeowners can now make more profit by utilizing services like Airbnb (renting out apartments to tourists for a few days can often generate more income than a tenant's monthly rent). So it's rearticulating what housing is for, and this is happening all across the world and here in Jackson.

If capital has international alliances and can dictate certain terms, we need to organize on an international level to counter these moves. This can enable us to restrict what rules these new businesses play by, and to ensure that our local communities are served by these new technologies. As part of this new municipalism, we want to create international networks that share experience, strategies, and build the organizational ties and political connections to gain more control over our lives. For us, this is the point of being involved in *Fearless Cities* and the whole municipalist movement. It's an effort to say that we need to be grounded locally, but also need deep international connections to have any impact on how capital moves and dictates our lives. It's a way of using the municipality as a concrete, tangible space where we can exercise our democratic rights to say, 'hey airbnb, hey uber,' if you would like to offer your services in Jackson these are the rules. And you can't just pick up your toys and play somewhere else as we have allies in London, Manchester, Barcelona, and Paris, who are also taking up the municipal mantel to place limits and boundaries on these new technologies. This is a key piece to why we, as Cooperation Jackson, engage with the broader municipal political platform.

JGF: While Black Liberation Movements have often been focused on civil rights—social gains—Cooperation Jackson has been working towards a 'democratic transformation of the economy.' Could you describe what a solidarity economy is?

KA: We say, in our case, that there are two levels to the solidarity economy in Jackson. The first level is really organic: it constitutes, particularly in poor communities, the core survival strategies that people have to deploy to exist. This entails a great deal of sharing in the form of cooking meals, providing transportation, and providing childcare for each other. These acts of solidarity do not expect financial compensation or reward, and are exchanges of what we can offer and have in abundance, most often our time.

In a place like Jackson, which has a population of roughly 200,000 people—more than 80% black—a quarter of the black population lives on or below the poverty line according to US living standards. With these economic constraints, the city's residents have to do a great deal of sharing and this is the basic elements of the organic solidarity economy. The limits to this, often, are that it only extends to kin networks, sharing with those people you know. I'm not criticizing these limits, but on a broader systemic level, and this is where Cooperation Jackson operates, we are trying to support communities to move beyond kin networks to circulate value in the economy and meet human needs through setting up institutions, such as timebanking. This means residents can share and meet needs with people they may not immediately know. This is the second element of the solidarity economy—sharing in an intentional way—that we try to bring to the table.

When we first started in the administration, despite our radical notions and history, we adopted a traditional orientation around job creation. Even though we had a solidarity economy framework, we were trying to address unemployment. Within two or three years of trying to create jobs, though, there was no comprehensive approach. We could get new businesses started, but our local economy couldn't support these businesses and couldn't pay a decent living wage, so they collapsed or failed. After this realization, we knew we had to shift our strategies, acknowledging that if we did everything that we planned successfully, it might create 20,000 jobs. But in Jackson, there is a concrete need for more than 80,000 jobs. So the 20,000 jobs, though not insignificant, would not resolve the problem. So if we couldn't provide jobs, we asked 'how do we do improve the quality of life?'

So Cooperation Jackson, at our current stage of development, is working through the solidarity economy, figuring out how to use these practices to improve the overall quality of life in a way that is not explicitly tied to creating jobs. It also means that cooperatives are just part of the toolkit and not the be-all and end-all of our solidarity economy.

JGF: Co-operatives are not just businesses, they are social movements. Is this what you mean when you've talked about 'politicizing' co-ops?

KA: This is very important. We start with the notion that a co-operative is a means of organizing working people. We infuse them with a very deliberate element of class consciousness. If you look at the history of co-ops in the US, they've been used in ways that are contrary to building a true solidarity economy. If you take some of the greatest perpetrators—such as the food co-ops of the 1970s and early 1980s—they were extensions of the worldview and lifestyle choices of the alternative, hippy generation who wanted to live more organically and holistically.

So they ended up creating these very specific niche, organic food markets that provided alternative goods. That had a good run for a while. But from the 1980s, sadly, to be able to afford organic products you needed an upper-class income. At the time co-ops were not thinking about how you could create organic products for mass distribution at affordable prices: 'How do we challenge big agriculture with affordable organic products?'

There is a deep politicization here as gentrification has created new dynamics in places like Brooklyn, NY, or Los Angeles, where I grew up, where people were opening new co-ops that did not serve the local community, just those with the disposable incomes to buy organic wheat or grass-fed meat. So politicizing co-ops would be to ask how we can create affordable organic products that can improve our health and lives through better eating. How do we extend that type of solidarity if we do not raise political questions or think of this as a challenge you have to solve.

This is a general example, but if we do not use politics to understand the oppression that affects our lives, we will often find as we grow and develop, our members will do well, but often at the expense of other around us. This breeds animosity and competition, which ultimately goes against our efforts to improve not only our own lives, but also those we want to work with. You have to address inequality and inequity as part of this new economic model, if we don't, we know from experience that we will reproduce and replicate the inequalities that come from the standard capitalist business model.

Possible Futures

Urban Sanctuary:
The Promise of Solidarity Cities

Antje Dieterich

As the sites of a shared lived experience, cities offer a unique opportunity to develop new political subjectivities that move beyond nationality and citizenship.

Sanctuary cities, solidarity cities, fearless cities, rebel cities—in recent years, we have witnessed the emergence of a new cycle of struggles around the theme of urban space in various parts of the Global North. For those in the United States, it is almost impossible not to have heard of sanctuary cities (where municipal authorities refuse full compliance with national immigration laws to offer limited shelter and public services to undocumented migrants and refugees), or at least of Donald Trump's threats to end federal funding for them. In Canada, the cities of London and Montréal recently declared themselves sanctuary cities as a direct reaction to Trump's xenophobic anti-immigration discourse.

The idea of the sanctuary city also extends to Europe, where it is attracting increasing attention from journalists and researchers alike. These developments clearly show how the notion of the sanctuary city has gained political salience, constituting a growing threat to the neoliberal and conservative order of things across the globe. It is this radical potential of sanctuary cities that motivated us to adopt the concept here in Berlin, trying to improve urban living conditions while simultaneously working on the further development of the political concept itself. The notion of the sanctuary city itself is flexible, depending on the needs and orientations of the communities pushing for it, which sometimes leaves it vulnerable to cooptation or sheer meaninglessness. But aside from the legitimate critiques and questions that can be raised, the potential of sanctuary cities to offer new organizational structures is promising enough to warrant a closer look.

Protection, Service, and Hospitality

If there is one common denominator behind the different municipalities that claim the mantle of sanctuary city, it is to make urban spaces safely accessible, independent of formal residency status. Beyond that, the shared attributes are very limited. In North America, for instance, some cities focus on ending the collaboration between federal deportation agencies and the local police. Others focus on municipal policies that allow "access without fear," so that undocumented migrants can access medical, educational and other social services without having to fear that the respective service providers will inform deportation agencies. Others still just seem to claim the title to signal that the city ambiguously aims for a non-racist living environment.

These differences are mirrored in the identities and strategies of the actors fighting to make their city a sanctuary city. In some places, the main protagonists are strong grassroots movements, pushing the city's government to implement protective legislations. The No One Is Illegal campaign in Toronto is one such example. In other places, the city's government declares the city a *de facto* sanctuary city without further legal changes. National City, California is an example of this approach. In others still, grassroots movements fight for a sanctuary city based on informal support structures, with the city's government actively opposing their efforts. Miami, Florida is currently an example of this type of case.

To understand the many differences and similarities, a short overview of the history and context of the concept of the sanctuary city is therefore helpful. The term sanctuary city can be found over many centuries, crossing state lines and religious divides and standing for some kind of protection within the city walls—often protection from oppression or persecution. The modern concept, however, was developed in the US as a reaction to increasingly restrictive migration policies and a rapid retreat of the social state. When the sanctuary movement first surged in the 1980s, explicitly left-wing political projects like the Black Panthers faced waves of violent police repression. This created a political vacuum that churches with left leanings could exploit, due the kind of discursive and legal protections they enjoy. So, when growing numbers of refugees began to arrive in the US as a result of the civil wars in Central America, these churches formed a sanctuary movement.

In the early years of the movement, religious communities simply offered first aid—shelter, food and the like. But with both faith-based community-building and the illegalization of migration on the rise, the step to provide further protection to migrant communities was not too far off. Throughout the 1990s the notion gradually developed into a more explicitly political concept, with different actors no longer just requesting shelter but increasingly claiming a right to full participation in the everyday life of the city.

Sanctuary Cities in Europe

In 2005, the political—rather than religious—concept made its way to Anglophone Europe, with an alliance of grassroots movements in Ireland and the UK pushing for collective urban hospitality for refugees, starting with the City of Sanctuary organization founded in Sheffield that year. By 2007, the activist platform had managed to implement the first legal changes in Sheffield and beyond.

In the next years, the concept spread to the European continent, where a variety of factors were radically changing the political landscape. For starters, the Arab Spring opened Europe's external borders to refugees and migrants from different African states, enabling large migration flows that had previously been held back by agreements between the EU and local dictators. At the same time, the countries where most refugees arrived—Greece, Italy and Spain—were hit particularly hard by the consequences of the global financial crisis. Due to the so-called Dublin Regulation, an EU law that regulates member-state responsibilities for asylum seekers, these countries were pretty much left to deal with the sudden increase in arrivals by themselves, even as they were forced to implement rigorous austerity programs, stripping their population of much-needed social security and public services.

These conditions in turn led to the development of different mutual aid projects and solidarity campaigns. Athens is known for its solidarity clinics, Barcelona developed solidarity housing projects, and Naples institutionalizes the cooperation with social movements—to name but a few. Throughout this process, the term *sanctuary* was sometimes replaced with the more fitting term *solidarity*. As in the US, the composition of social forces behind these different sanctuary and solidarity cities varies widely. The mayor of Naples, for instance, seeks to enable a diversity of solidarity initiatives, the anarchist movement in Athens runs self-managed squats, and different social movement organizations in Barcelona are participating in the local government.

In all of these cities, however, new initiatives emerged that did not focus purely on undocumented people, but on *all* people who are excluded from the everyday life of the city. It is this imaginary of solidarity that is currently also animating our municipal project in Berlin.

Conditions in Germany: Between Image and Reality

Living an illegalized life in Germany is very hard, if not impossible, to accomplish. Legal and historical developments created a particular terrain for refugees and, with it, for solidarity city initiatives. Spoiler alert: Germany has a history of xenophobia. "Not to be a land of immigration" was, for the longest time, part of the country's national identity—also after the war. Even when programs were developed to attract foreign workers, needed for the rapidly growing industry of the 1950s and 1960s, these workers were defined as "guest workers" (in the West) or "contractors" (in the East) who were expected to leave after their work in Germany was completed. As a result, both German states followed exceedingly strict policies of segregation and ghettoization.

The anti-immigration state discourse is reflected in legal conditions that are relevant for the solidarity city concept. It starts with Germany's blood-bond citizenship, as opposed to the soil-bond citizenship of the United States, that makes it very hard for people to leave the precarious status of illegality through a safety net built by families. Another obstacle is the asylum legislation. Although the right is established in the constitution, it is nearly impossible to be granted asylum in today's Germany. Since the early 1990s, any person who entered a "safe third country" before reaching Germany will be deported back to that state. What this means in practice is that, if you did not manage to get a direct flight from your respective homeland in crisis to Germany, including all the required papers, stamps and visa, the German state will do everything in its power to prevent you from establishing an existence here. And the state's tools are simple: it refuses to provide work permits, limits freedom of movement to a single municipality (sometimes a state), blocks access to education, and provides only very limited and defective shelter, often in isolated large camps.

The combination of the long-standing segregation between migrant and non-migrant communities and the extreme restrictions faced by asylum-seekers and refugees in everyday life creates extreme obstacles to successful self-organization. And yet despite these challenges, refugees began to massively self-organize around 2013 (although there had been various attempts before that time, they mostly did not reach the same level of success). One of the most important steps in 2013 was to move from the remote camps provided by the state into the city centers. Churches, squares, parks, monuments and abandoned school buildings became the spaces where asylum-seekers and refugees established a new social visibility. From there, the struggle grew exponentially: by 2015, as millions of refugees and undocumented migrants arrived on Europe's shores, every city in the country had some kind of welcoming initiative. The emergency shelters closed their doors to volunteers as there were just too many. On the night of September 4, these solidarity efforts went viral when Angela Merkel and her Austrian counterpart let trains full of refugees pass the borders from Hungary for one day.

So, all's well that ends well, then? Hardly. While the pictures of welcoming Germans looked good on camera, the reality was quite different. Every small concession that refugees and undocumented people—along with their supporters—obtained was answered with a hard backlash: less than three weeks after Merkel supposedly opened the borders, the federal government implemented another set of cutbacks on the right to asylum, leading to mass deportations of ethnic minorities to the newly defined "safe states" of Albania, Montenegro and Kosovo, where many had suffered from violent oppression.

There are countless examples for such back-and-forths. In January 2015, limitations on the freedom of movement were abolished, only to be re-introduced in November, this time with the possibility to immediately deport people who leave their designated municipality more than once. Similar developments took place over the past two years, with changes in allowances, access to education, special protection for unaccompanied minors, and so on. The latest reform from May 2017 introduces massive invasions into the privacy of refugees (such as random cellphone searches), increased "detention pending deportation" and ankle monitors. These legal changes are small steps in a long and ongoing process towards the total abolition of the right to asylum in Germany. Despite huge waves of support and sympathy from society, the actual legal conditions for the vast majority of refugees have dramatically worsened over the last years.

Solidarity City Berlin

It has become clear, then, that even mass mobilizations in solidarity with refugees were not enough to get us anywhere. The state has adapted to our tactics: demonstrations were simply allowed to move peacefully through the city, slowing down traffic here and there, but not leading to any real political change. The squatting of an old school building provoked a short, extreme reaction, but when the state realized that eviction was not a feasible option it changed its strategy, waiting the squatters out until public attention passed on.

With a federal government that had time on its side, and successfully developed a façade of "caring" about refugees, we, too, needed a new idea, a new discourse, a new strategic response. With cities in Southern Europe struggling for solidarity in times of extreme austerity, and with North American movements working on strategies to protect their undocumented community members, we had good examples for the development of a new battle plan; one that focuses on the right to move, live, learn or work in our city. We "simply" had to adapt these ideas to our local conditions.

We quickly discovered that, within our city and our everyday lives produced in it, we are able to find answers to very general political questions, such as the issue of political subjectivity under the conditions of social fragmentation produced by neoliberalism. The subjectivity we aim to mobilize is simply our neighbors—people who live in the same urban space. We don't have to construct a shared history, because we define our "we" through our shared everyday space. Some definitions change with this new strategy, first of all the divisions between refugees, undocumented people and citizens. With the changes in asylum legislation, it is only a matter of time until many refugees become illegalized—but beyond that, we share many problems experienced in our everyday lives relating to the consequence of austerity, gentrification or even changes in labor laws.

With this less strict separation of actors comes the understanding that deportations, as executions of German national asylum legislation, are just part of the wider problem that we identify as European neoliberalism. With its need for surplus labor it leads to the erosion of the social state, workers' protections and affordable housing, forces people to move from the South to the North, and leaves us all to fight over the bread crumbs. In short: among our neighbors, we can find a variety of oppressed groups that quite often share very similar experiences of everyday life in the city.

What we needed for this idea to become a useful strategy was a formalized space to develop more concrete ideas. With the help of comrades from No One Is Illegal in Toronto we created this space through the formation of an alliance. Its member organizations, largely consisting of refugees and undocumented people, remained focused on questions around a precarious residency status—not because we think that residency is the only problem people face, but because it is a factor that makes many other fights harder. In debates and inquiries, we began to identify that the most important fields for the undocumented and refugees in our alliance could be divided into five fields: health, education, work, housing and protection from and by the law.

We then decided to develop policy proposals for each of these issue areas, answering the questions: "What are the concrete problems?" and "What would concrete solutions for these problems in Berlin look like?" Answering these questions involved doing research and it also meant looking for small, possible reforms. Beginning with the issue area of health, we have so far reached a pretty clear understanding of the possibilities to provide healthcare coverage for everyone in Berlin, including some clear and simple outlines for a potential system to be put in place.

A Model of Urban Self-Governance

By producing concrete proposals, we are able to approach political decision-makers and force them to position themselves around our key demand. "No borders, no nations?" All for it. But the mayor of Berlin isn't, and most people have no way to imagine a world without nations. Denying children the ability to receive healthcare, on the other hand, is much harder to sell to your electorate. With the understanding that our community consists of all our neighbors, we then make this unifying idea a guideline for further research. We try to develop policy proposals that, first, do not allow for a separation based on residency status, and second, serve as stepping stones to make the voice of social movements heard, in order to better protect ourselves from the backlashes that have tainted past successes.

For health, this involves demanding universal coverage for people without insurance, whether they are undocumented, come from another European state, or have just fallen through the cracks of the system for whatever reason. It also means that we want to participate in a newly developed institution, like an advisory board composed of neighbors and social actors. This allows us to consolidate our achievements in healthcare provision but also to slowly co-construct a more participatory form of urban self-governance. If local institutions become more and more democratically controlled, this in return allows for further social mobilization and the participation of larger groups of people in local politics. Our horizon for Berlin would therefore be to develop a complex of participatory institutions that allow us to learn, live and work in our future sanctuary.

With similar problems all over Europe and beyond, parallel ideas developed. Terms such as *cities of change, rebel cities* or *solidarity cities* stand for different attempts to connect cities with similar imaginations of a radical urban future. Instead of running against slow and powerful federal governments or trying to change the neoliberal base of the European Union, the idea is to create something like a confederation of cities, pushing for change outside or rather parallel to larger governmental structures. Such attempts have an extensive history in Europe, where cities have long been the place of liberation, sanctuary, and yes, citizenship. If we take into account the fact that 70-75 percent of the European population lives in urban spaces, it is not too hard to imagine that important changes will be effected by this key demographic. Cities, to us, are the first step—or a parallel move, rather—in a broader conquest of democracy that can eventually begin to erode the nation-state and the European Union as we know it.

Sounds more like a dream of the future? Absolutely, but it is a dream worth fighting for—and one that can be divided into small, feasible steps. Perhaps we shouldn't even call it a dream, but rather a political horizon we can work towards together. With such a shared horizon in our minds we can—and should—begin to coordinate our different efforts, contextualize the local fights we win and put these small victories to work within our larger frame.

"Urban Sanctuary: The Promise of Solidarity Cities" was originally published in *Roar Magazine*, Issue #6 (Summer 2017): 48-60.

How Hip-Hop Can Save Us

Austin Krauss

In my day-dreams the following is painted large on a wall, just inside the entrance to some old brick building, against which children are filing past:

---

7 Principles of The Cypher

1. Money buys nothing & bosses are whack.

2. Everyone gets to express themselves.

3. Nobody is forced to do something they don't want to do.

4. You inspire the growth & morale of everyone else.

5. You are responsible for deciding who you want to be.

6. Together, we decide what we want to be.

7. The Cypher is Family.

If you agree to try and learn the above principles you may enter these doors.

And may all those who have embodied these principals carry them far beyond the bounds of these walls.

Hip-Hop will save the world.

Hip-Hop Will Save the World...?

I live just outside the city of Albany, NY. It's a beautiful, ugly, little city, which is also the seat of our state's corruption-prone capital, attendant with hideous, Rockefeller-mandated architecture. We have above average murder rates, solid public transportation, and a downright notable chicken joint at the top of South Pearl St. We also have plentiful abandoned buildings—the remnants of our bygone industrial glory and absconded working class—on which to project one's daydreams. For instance, on 2nd and Thornton St. there is an old public school with overgrown courtyards and boarded windows, which—in my daydreams—has been resurrected.

I see only a bustling silhouette as shapes pass in and out of the doorway and shuffle around in the shaded courtyards. But as I listen to the unmistakable sound of two turntables and the unseen hands of a DJ, deftly recomposing the wreckage of the past, it seems apparent that a new curriculum is in effect. I listen as the sounds carry down to the sidewalk below, where some kids have gathered in a circle against the graffitied facade. Inside the swaying circle is a single girl. Caught in the rhythm, she is everywhere at once. And indeed, the rhythm seems to be coming straight from her soul. Just as the beat cuts her feet shoot up into the air, and for a moment, as all the world revolves in the palm of her hand, time stands still.

I take a look down the sidewalk, and all down the tag-riddled concrete they are gathered in circles as they study, share, and build. Their projects of wood, cloth, clay, metal, and glass clutter the alleys, spilling out from the workshops and into the place where the street used to be, but where people now philosophize in the shade of chestnut trees. It's a place where work, art, and play all run up against each other and become one. Where everything bears the imperfect beauty that is the mark of a human hand. Because, from their buildings and ships and down to the tops of the bottoms of their toilet lids, everything they lay their potent hands upon, they adorn with color, virtue, and humanity. When the sun sets, they leave their various instruments and tools laid neatly along the sidewalks and retire to their stoops where, above their heads, luxuriant gardens bathed in a numinous light hang down over the roof-tops of the row houses, which are splashed with murals for as far as the eye can see. The last resonance of their theories and dreams echo down the corridors and carry off into the aether—and then I wake up.

Me? I mostly dig holes for a living. But, between my daydreams and the exigencies of life, I observe a culture known as Hip-Hop. Hip-hop is composed of four practices or "elements": Graffiti writing, DJing, MCing, and breaking. The graphic, musical, verbal, and physical components of a unified cultural movement. For my part, I practice the element of breaking. I'm a b-boy. Along with my crew, I try my best to pass down this culture and this art as faithfully as I can. I teach at schools and community centers, in studios and on sidewalks. I get personal satisfaction and not much else. In my daydreams, they don't need much else. They come from far and wide to get down in our cypher, lay hands on the wall of the 7 Principles, and never doubt of what they do. In my daydreams, they are true believers.

Hip-Hop, They Believe, Will Save the World...

Just what is hip-hop? It is many things to many people. But for now it's sufficient to know that, as KRS-One frames it, "hip-hop is something you live."

Live? What a novelty in our age of mass shootings, impending ecological catastrophe, and the necrophilia that is our infatuation with iPhone. Smack in the middle of this culture of passive spectatorship, morbid consumption, and an ever-more suicidal nihilism—a culture all-but-conquered by the way of death—and here we got this thing you "live"? In so many ways, it seems that all we any longer want is simply not to *be*. But the problem of nihilism is, in some ways, a very simple one: it is simply a matter of getting people to want to be alive again.

The origin myth of Hip-Hop is simple enough. In the beginning, there is chaos. A state of ceaseless and inarticulate violence brought on by a policy of "benign neglect," the active, state-sponsored obliteration of entire neighborhoods, and the merciless snuffing out of every aspiration we once held dear. This is the South Bronx circa 1970—devastation, disunity, and death. Yet, it is out of this—out of chaos and nothingness—that peace, unity, and a culture of inexhaustible creativity suddenly burst into being. The turning point can perhaps be isolated to the death of an individual known as "Black Benji" who is killed while attempting to arbitrate a gang dispute, the tragic circumstances of which—in conjunction with a generalized fatigue with violence—culminate in an event known as the Hoe Avenue Meeting, out of which a peace treaty is brokered, Dec, 8th 1971, reconciling the gangs of South Bronx. Forthwith a period of unprecedented cultural exchange ensues as territorial barriers are lifted, which—in conjunction with a generalized mood of celebration—will manifest in some of the founding jams of hip-hop. Many once-violent gangs join in these celebrations, sublimating their aggressive and tribal energy into the new and peaceful forms, subsequently reforming their gangs into hip-hop crews, which then proceed to spreading this new way—the way of life—to the rest of the world. Life triumphs over death. Jeff Chang said that "Living young and free in the Bronx was a revolutionary act of art. To unleash on a social level these vital urges was the surest way to ward off mass death."[1]

We ought to celebrate this triumph—always and in all ways—but there is a price. Even as we walk this lofty tight-wire that is human passion, venturing to be alive—sincerely, un-ironically, un-abashedly, and all-the-way live!—we can never be permitted to delude ourselves in what lies beneath. We can never be permitted to forget what we came from. From our militant stance down to the slant of our hats, the residue of our past is writ into our every gesture and word, forever to be exorcised, symbolically and ritualistically, in "battle." Because violence (and, for that matter, injustice) is not defused by peace, but only by a tireless devotion to the enforcement of respect, caution, and the mutual preservation of dignity. This is what it means to be a b-boy. This is the vigil we maintain, lest we plunge backward into that barbarism and disunity from which we came, and which remains, ever-present, just beneath the surface of everyday civility. This is the price of life. Indeed, it is precisely this cosmologic-backdrop, what the Greek philosopher Castoriadis called the imaginary of chaos, which is the prerequisite of life.[2]

If we imagine that we originate from a universe where everything is already as it ought to be—i.e. where all is justly-ordered by some benevolent force (what is now our eminently logical state, and its sublimely efficient economy)— than what need is there for us to get involved? Indeed, if we truly believe this, then there is nothing left for us to do but obey. But if, on the other hand, it is understood that the universe is perpetual chaos, and that life has no intrinsic order or meaning—other than what we give to it—than we might as well get up and build something together in the short time we are here. This, coincidentally, is the same imaginary which gave rise to the political form known as democracy. In both cases, what is understood here is that the "Gods" are not going to be looking out for us mere mortals. It is left to us to make the world how we see fit.

In my daydream, politics is something that happens afternoons on the stoop, between puffs of tobacco, and sips of dandelion wine. Or,

Sunday mornings in the inner-blocks as little kids chase hens around the meeting circle. Indeed, it is something deeply intimate, an occasion of ritual and ceremony. Gifts are exchanged, feasts are planned, births announced, and new people are initiated and welcomed into the community. It is something from which they derive a sense of potency, purpose, and belonging, as they convene their neighborhood assemblies at the parks and ratify their agreements under the hallowed rims of basketball courts. Every voice is heard. Every thought valid. Everyone is, in some small way, a hero. They carve the doors with their triumphant mythologies, and glaze every vessel with the scenes of their everyday, heroic deeds. And as they deliberate atop their high places, looking out over their city like gods, their children sit atop their shoulders, watching as their mothers and fathers proceed to make this world how they see fit.

As C.L.R James once put it, "Every cook can govern."[3] Here, in my daydreams, everyone is a cook. Everyone is a politician, custodian, musician, teacher, artist, agronomist, craftsman, and philosopher all in the course of a day. In short, they are complete human beings. Because this is their measure of wealth. They believe in the development of every single person to their fullest human potential, and the first thing they teach their children is hip-hop.

Between my daydreams and the exigencies of life, I teach kids the art and culture of hip-hop. I love what I do. I try to believe in what I do. But there have been days where my faith runs up against an impasse. How do you teach the foot-slide to a kid with no shoes? How do you tell a girl whose dad is locked-up and whose mom is working three jobs to keep practicing her breath control? How do you ask a young man who has no certain future—indeed, a young man who is not even sure there will be dinner tonight—to do another windmill? You can't eat windmills.

I suppose this is the part where I swat away the fog of my daydreams and start being realistic. Hip-hop alone cannot save the world.

Also, to be clear, I am not much of a b-boy. I do not do this for any obvious reason. I do not do this under the sanction of local authority, or on the advice of my high-school career counselor. I don't even do this because I'm particularly good at it! Nah. The reason I do it is because I'd lose my damn mind if I didn't do it. That is, because I need to. And because fuck you if you don't like it! Self-expression is not something reserved for professionals. It is not the province of the talented or the cultured. It is not an aptitude, a privilege, or an innate gift. It is a universal right. Human beings *must* express themselves. Everyone has the right to be an artist and to exercise their creative agency within the space of their community. This is the achieved reality of Hip-Hop. The gallery is now antiquated and the stage obsolete. Hip-Hop has democratized art.

Why do I do it? I do it because the greatest feeling I know is the moment when a kid sees me do it and suddenly believes that they can do it too. And, though it may never put cereal in their bowls or shoes on their feet, this has not seemed to stop the countless little b-boys and girls who, on empty stomachs and with feet bared, light up the dim corners of this world with a passion for this culture and a will-to-life too pure for any of my words to ever express. Indeed, if you were not aware, this is the largest art movement the world has ever seen—by far. It has spread to nearly every corner of the globe and syncretized with all the cultures of the world. It has become a sort of global indigenous culture weaving us together under a common rhythm, as it daily brings the most diverse and disparate of peoples into a commerce once unfathomable. It is a language which precedes words. A language without which, for me at least, words have no meaning. And, without such a language there is no hope of engaging the world in any meaningful way. So, if you'll permit me, I will press on in this attempt to put into these lifeless words what can only be lived.

I write the following not as an academic or anthropologist but as someone who participates in this culture and has felt the stir of this language, however faintly, from the inside. If b-boying has taught me anything, it is that a whole universe of possibility is opened if only you renounce the arrogance of being upright, if only you embrace the quadruped we all once were. By the same token, the limitless potential of second nature can only be unlocked by facing the limits of our first nature. Human beings are aggressive, egotistical and tribalistic. Hip-hop neither runs from it, nor submits to it. Rather, it sublimates this vital energy into a peaceful and creative mode of expression, which is both cooperative and competitive without being violent or hierarchical. This presents an evolutionary development in modern human culture. Here is a mode of culture where the rules adhere to us instead of the other way around. In hip-hop, any given battle is but a skirmish in the larger style war, and style is less about being "the best" as it is about scouting your niche and displacing the center of what is "hip." Strength, speed, intelligence and technical ability are not the ultimate assurance of success here. In the end it is the one who is able to get open—to connect with the rhythm, and themselves, in the most uninhibited and creative manner—who ultimately triumphs. And, indeed, here is where the divide between mind and body begins to dissolve.

In hip-hop "Knowledge" is not strictly cerebral. Hipness is knowledge which is carried in the body, itself. Therefore, the "hop" here is not simply denoting movement, but a particular mode of movement. It is, manifestly, a leap. In so many ways, it is a leap of faith. Because whenever we muster the courage to get open—to reach out and mark a wall, or lay hands on a moving record, or touch hand to ground, or otherwise let the rhythm take hold as words and movements flow freely from somewhere we can never be sure—we enact one of these metaphysical gestures and affirm a sort of militant optimism, which is at once a faith in our-self, as it is an act of profound solidarity. "I rebel, therefore we are" as Camus stated it.[4] And everywhere that true hip-hop is practiced, it is predicated on that idea. On the conviction that there exists a larger community whose existence we may indeed never be certain of, but which our active belief in actually has the affect of willing into existence! This is the faith of every kid who ever ventured out anonymously into the night to throw his tag on a wall. This is the beginning of all community. As Schloss wrote, "One must project an absolute certainty that, if one does something valuable, no matter how subtle, it will be appreciated."[5]

A leap can never be assured. And yet everywhere you will find that this leap of hip-hop is intended to look effortless—a mere hop. It is confident, but a sort of confidence which is pulled straight out of air. What is understood here is that you must provisionally fake it in order to make it. But the miraculous thing about this dialogic of hip and hop is that the further it carries, the further it confirms that boundless potentiality which was, at first, posited merely as an article of faith. This is how we realize our greatest selves. This is self-creation.

Knowledge here is inseparable from the body; it is confidence, it is self-respect, and, indeed, it is the ability to determine and even create oneself out of thin air! I call this peculiar sort of knowledge bodily wisdom, and it seems to me that it is the necessary foundation for any other sort of wisdom that we hope to follow. For it may well be easy to imagine a good life, and to sight the path that might take us there. But what good is knowing even the best of paths if we do not have the confidence to walk it? What good is knowing even the best sort of life, if there is not-yet a people capable of living it? I believe that Hip-Hop can make such a people.

Rancier wrote that "Equality is not given, nor is it claimed; it is practiced, it is verified."[6] In Hip-Hop culture, the place where this occurs is the cypher. It is simply a circle, composed of people, who have gathered, spontaneously, to dance or rhyme. The participants of the cypher take turns, in random order, freestyling to the music, playing off of, and responding to whoever preceded them. The free entry into the cypher is inhibited only by one's courage and preparedness to participate, and if one cypher does not suit you, you can make your own! Ultimately, the cypher is a space of play, but the virtues of this play are profound. Once again, there is a sort of wisdom at work here which is baked into the very structure and functioning of this culture, and which finds its essence in the virtue of a circle. The cypher begins with something held in common: when something is held in common, there is community, and in community there is communication, and with this arises participation. Because without participation there can be no equality, and without the unqualified equality of all, there is no freedom for anyone. In one sweeping motion, the cypher realizes all of this. It instills democracy at the most fundamental and organic level, the level of interpersonal relationships, and it imbues this wisdom in the body as a lived practice—cultural democracy.

And there it is again; that D-word. Could it be that there is some invisible thread across the ages, binding Ancient Greece to the South Bronx? As it was with Athenian democracy, the chief fault of Hip-Hop lies not in Hip-Hop itself but has only ever been in how we define a legitimate participant. Simply stated, we must cease to qualify participation. It is my conviction that the only way to circumvent the ceaseless antagonism and inevitable violence which identity politics has conjured, is to establish a common identity around that which is inessential, i.e. that which can be universalized. Only culture can do this. In the end, only an identity rooted in culture holds the promise of overcoming, if not our differences themselves, then the inevitable antagonism that must come of founding identify on that which can never be universalized.

At its essence, Hip-Hop is the art of aligning rhythms and nothing achieves this more ecstatically than the cypher. It is one of the only spaces in which culture supersedes identity without destroying it. One must let the subconscious take hold in the heat of a freestyle; it cannot help but tell the truth of that person. The cypher is uniquely, perhaps solely, suited to deal, in a democratic venue, with man on his interior level—as opposed to the exterior, which is what political artifice deals in. It is in this fashion, by way of countless battles and small victories that are no less glorious for their being small, that culture can succeed in transcending ethnicity, race, gender and class as the basis of identity. Here is a space that operates on our scale—a human scale. Here is the potential for all of us to make ourselves felt in the world.

Can Hip-Hop Save the World?

No. Only we can do that. The question is, can hip-hop create a "we"? More precisely, can cultural democracy prefigure political democracy? For Joe Schloss, the promise of hip-hop, is that we might "exercise control over the meaning, value, and direction of [our] lives." If this is true, then the promise of hip-hop is politics.

Outside my daydreams politics is self-abasement. It consists of the convoluted and humiliating process of surrendering power every 4 years—the only true power we have being to willfully dis-empower ourselves. This we are told is "democracy." True democracy is the very inverse of this, our top-down system. Indeed it is so opposite anything you and I have ever known that few, outside my daydreams, would recognize it. It has nothing to do with representatives, or parties, or campaigns, or ossified ideologies, or anything that takes place under the columns of some lobbyist-infested senate. Real democracy comes from the stoop. It was born on the streets and in the courtyards, at the workshops and in the fields, in the kitchens and in the classrooms. It sprang up in countless places, at countless times all though history. And why? Because nothing was there to stop it. And though it has gone by many names throughout history, it is always the same; a mass of people coming together as equals to determine their own destiny. As it currently stands, this project has poked its head back up under the name of Municipalism. Murray Bookchin maintained that "The overriding problem is to change the structure of society so that people gain power. The best arena to do that is the municipality—the city, town, and village—where we have an opportunity to create face-to-face democracy."[7]

States can never be democratic. They are inhuman, distant things, held together by force and cynicism. It can never be known except by the vapidness of its symbols or the sting of its rod. Cities are different. We can know our city. We can know its streets and neighborhoods. We can know its people, and name its problems from personal experience. And because we can know it, we can govern it. This is the original meaning of Politics, which, for the Greeks, meant the affairs of the cities. To believe in the city is to believe in the potential of human-beings to achieve something together. It is the place of possibility.

Up to now, libertarian municipalism is a politics without a culture. For a long while, Hip-hop has been a culture searching for a politics. The definitive urban culture, and the superlative urban politics; if either of them is to succeed, it is here in the city where they must meet. With this union we can begin to envision a society where hip-hop takes on a vital portion of the task of reforming our passive citizenship into one that is actively participatory. Which is to say, a society where hip-hop forms the basis of a new *paideia*, another one of those dusty Greek words. What it means is an education intended to create engaged citizens. What the Greeks understood was that there was no political democracy without a people capable of participating in it, and for them, curiously enough, citizenship began in the gymnasium. Under Athenian democracy all education began with the training and articulation of the body and the senses so as to appreciate rhythm, harmony and form. Only then did it expand out into intellectual and political fields. If it is true that there is no political democracy which is not first prefigured by cultural democracy, then *paideia* is the bridge which spans them. What gymnastics and poetry were to ancient education, DJing, B-Girling, MCing and Graffiti Writing can be today.

Politics, like hip-hop, is a discipline. It takes practice and active acculturation. If we are not capable of it, as of now—capable of its practice or etiquette, or of making informed decisions—it is only because we have been deliberately stunted and stultified. But, though we cannot see it from this shore, and indeed may not even know what it looks like, I believe that if we build this bridge from the right spot, it can make the place we wish to reach. Hip-hop can give our children the confidence to cross this bridge, but we have to find within ourselves the will to build it. It's left to us.

I suppose we—and by "we" I mean of course my imaginary constituency, which is growing larger by the moment—will inevitably face the charge of indoctrinating the youth, or some other such unsavory business! But I charge that this charge is dishonest. We are already indoctrinating the youth. From the earliest age we steep them in the pathologies of shame, deferral and escape. We teach them that common people aren't capable of thinking for themselves; that you shouldn't bother with something unless you can get paid; unless you're a professional; unless you can be "the best." We train them to eternally defer their life to some later date—which never quite arrives—and to willingly forfeit their labour to some dream—which is not quite their own—scratching furiously at lottery-ticket hopes, as the seeds of tomorrow go unplanted. Worst of all!? We teach them to be ashamed of where it is they come from. We tell them not to bother with their cities and neighborhoods—that their slums and ghettos are not worth fixing. That all we can hope to do is get away.

It is left to us to decide. Do we want to continue to tell our children to keep their heads down and plod on, watching as they slowly drown their hopes in the shallow pool of *realism*? Are we content to hand them down an ever-more narrow future? Watching, in turn, as they hand down even less, until one day there is simply not much left to hand down? Or, do we want to make a break? Because what if I said I don't want to get away? Indeed, what if I said I loved my slum? What if I said I wanted to make of this place a paradise?

Last month a man by the name of Elijah Cancer was shot and killed while attempting to break up a fight in Albany's South End. He too was a peace keeper. A former drug dealer and ex-con, he had decided to turn from the way of death and, with naked hands, he died shielding us from it. I've been thinking about this a lot lately. Thinking about myths and martyrs, about the angels of history, and the endless heap of trauma from which we must go on building this world. Thinking about how just as it was the immense destruction of the Cross-Bronx Expressway, forever cutting a jagged scar down the middle of that place, giving birth to this myth of hip-hop—giving birth to the thing I so love—so too, we have our own scars.

"Your City, Your Future!"

According to Albany's 2030 Executive Summary, "The City of Albany is a system that operates within a hierarchy of systems.... Your city, your future." In Albany, we have the Empire State Plaza. From its sun-blotting-scale, to its fortress-like walls and elevated detachment from surrounding neighborhoods, the Plaza represents everything about the state that is antithetical to democracy. A meticulously manicured parkway leads directly into the structure, giving a cozy, sanitized commute to its favored population of incoming bureaucrats and tourists, who snap selfies against the middle-finger-esque architecture for which 8,000 locals were evicted and their homes obliterated to make way. This massive and sublimely alienating structure sports—among other things—vast empty spaces, a McDonalds, and a collection of supremely uninspiring art. But at its very center—effectively obstructing any public gatherings—is a vast pool of dark, depthless water, which yet perfectly clarifies, to crystalline opaqueness, the central statement of this place. This is not our city. And yet for all that is wrong with it, there is but one thing absent to keep this plaza from being the hill of our future democracy—*us*. Here, Hannah Arendt's critical insight can guide us: "It is futile to search for an absolute to break the vicious cycle in which all beginning is inevitably caught, because this 'absolute' lies in the very act of beginning itself."[8]

For the Greeks, the original meaning of the word "idiot" was a person who did not participate in politics. As it is, we are all vapid idiots. But, maybe, somewhere along the line, we start teaching our kids to dream. Maybe we put pens in their hands, and begin inspiring each other to imagine not just a better neighborhood but the best of all possible neighborhoods. That is, maybe we propose the utility of eutopia[9]—the utility of imaging a better way of life. Maybe we decide that a democratically engaged citizenry necessitates not only being well informed, but participating in the processing and production of information. And because learning to articulate oneself is part and parcel of a civic education, maybe we decide to establish publications produced by our youth, in which they contribute. Maybe we call one of these publications Cypher Blossoms—maybe this becomes the platform for our ideas and dreams. Maybe we put out a call for everyone to contribute and to bring their own personal eutopias (written or spoken) to be workshopped in cyphers—drafting the pieces not as fiction, but as blueprints for a possible society (coincidentally, maybe this is the pretext by which we implement face-to-face democratic decision making in our communities). Maybe we begin trying to synthesis our eutopias into a collective charter (maybe this becomes the pretext by which we federate our neighborhoods). Maybe, with charter in hand, we begin to seize upon our symbolic spaces and lay our rightful claim to the high grounds, rededicating them to the city, instead of the empire. Appropriating the empty concourses and podiums for our jams, festivals, and general assemblies. Overwhelming the lifeless documents of their planning committees with the brilliance of our own collective vision as we declare, once and for all, "OUR City! OUR Future!"

Maybe then! Maybe. Because when the necessary elements are established—when a new rhythm animates our streets, and the art of our children covers our sidewalks and walls—it is then that the cyphers will blossom, and the renaissance may begin! And as it spreads forth, the ways of death will retreat in proportion, and give way to new life. Because, once we have a culture which prefigures the sort of politics in which we determine our own fate—in which we can choose to municipalize our economy and guarantee food, clothing and education to our children—maybe I won't have this little problem anymore. And then, just maybe, I can tell my students to do another windmill.

Endnotes

1 Jeff Chang, *Can't Stop, Won't Stop: A History of the Hip-Hop Generation* (New York: St. Martin's Press, 2005).

2 Cornelius Castoridis, *TheImaginary Institution of Society* (Cambridge: Polity Press, 1997).

3 C.L.R. James, "Every Cook can Govern,"*Correspondence,* Vol. 2, No. 12, June 1956.

4 Albert Camus, *The Rebel: An Essay on Man in Revolt* (New York: Random House, 1991).

5 Joseph Schloss, *Foundation: B-boys, B-girls and Hip-Hop Culture in New York* (Oxford: Oxford University Press, 2009).

6 Jacques Ranciere, *The Ignorant Schoolmaster: Five Lessons in Intellectual Emancipation* (Stanford: Stanford University Press, 1991).

7 Murray Bookchin, *The Next Revolution: Popular Assemblies & the Promise of Direct Democracy* (London: Verso, 2015).

8 Hannah Arendt, *On Revolution* (New York: The Viking Press, 1963).

9 I distinguish here between Utopia ("No-place") and its original Greek, Eutopia ("Good-place"). That said, their status as interchangeable homophones says something essential about eutopia: for it exists only in our perpetual pursuit of it.

From Social Ecology to Community Economies: Towards Better Livelihoods[1]

Anna Kruzynski

"We accept the premise that we live in an era of unprecedented and rapid environmental and social change. The recent 10,000-year history of climatic stability on Earth that enabled the rise of agriculture and domestication, the growth of cities, numerous technological revolutions, and the emergence of modernity is now over. We accept that in the latest phase of this era, modernity is unmaking the stability that enabled its emergence. Over the 21st century, severe and numerous weather disasters, scarcity of key resources, major changes in environments, enormous rates of extinction, and other forces that threaten life are set to increase. But we are deeply worried that current responses to these challenges are focused on market-driven solutions and thus have the potential to further endanger our collective commons."

— Katherine Gibson, Deborah Bird Rose and Ruth Fincher,
"Preface," *Manifesto for Living in the Anthropocene*[2]

This text is a thought experiment. Rather than working with ideological labels, I want to do some mental gymnastics with methods and concepts that inspire me. To work towards an organizing method that is both inspiring (better livelihoods are possible) and anchored in pragmatism. I will start by sharing my understanding of the exploitation and oppression of humans and nature. Then, I will reflect on the ideas put forth by Murray Bookchin and on the application of the concepts of social ecology and libertarian municipalism by the anarchist collective La Pointe libertaire. After that, I will address J.K. Gibson-Graham's notions of diverse economies and community economies, as well as the position of the Community Economies Collective (CEC) on social change. Finally, I will come back to Pointe-Saint-Charles to propose a concrete application of these ideas, a method of organisation. My aim here is not to convince, but to spark debate with others working towards building better livelihoods.

Exploitation and Oppression

I firmly believe that while difference ought to be celebrated, hierarchies must be fought. This idea that men are better than women, cis-gendered people are better than trans people, that white skin is better than black skin, that heterosexuality is better than homosexuality, that being thin is better than being fat. This idea is propagated by schools, the media, families, social and health services, religious institutions. This idea that materializes through dynamics of domination. Because those who benefit from this stratification often find themselves in roles where they are making decisions that affect all of us. They control the production of goods and services that we need to live (survive). They take hostage our security, our physical and psychological integrity.

I believe that the organisation of society perpetuates this stratification (naturalizes it) and is the basis for the exploitation of humans and nature.

All humans work. A good number work eight hours or more per day to get what they need to survive (a wage) and to produce wealth for, more often than not, owners or shareholders of firms. Nature also contributes to this wealth: minerals, non-renewable energies, soil fertility, vegetable and animal species. Wealth stems from the theft of the planet's reserves and from workers' labour. And it is the bosses who decide how that wealth is distributed. Often, these same bosses sail the Caribbean in their luxury yachts while the planet is destroyed and humans struggle to survive.

This is exploitation.

That is not all. Humans, even once home, are not finished working. Doing groceries, weeding the garden, preparing meals, doing dishes, laundry, dusting, sweeping up, washing the windows, disinfecting the toilet, helping their loved ones, helping with homework, participating in the general assembly of the women's centre, mediating, calling the Housing Board, paying bills.... Who does this unpaid work? This invisible, free, work that benefits the entire family, the community, and society at large? Overwhelmingly, it is women. This is exploitation. This is not all. Humans, overworked, in survival mode, buy what they need where it costs the least and, ideally, where they can buy it all at once. But what lies behind the low prices of the Walmarts and Costcos of the world? A plethora of other humans who work in distant lands for miserable salaries in terrible conditions, these other humans who live in the global South, or in poor and racialized neighbourhoods in Northern cities. And an exploited planet that can barely breathe. The survival of humans is dependent on that of other humans and of the natural environment. The exploitation of one fuels the exploitation of the other.

This is not all. Overworked humans and the exhausted planet are squeezed even more by continued enclosure or non-management of commons[3]—knowledge, property or practice—that is shared by a community. While biophysical commons are stolen and exploited by capitalists at the head of multinational corporations, Indigenous protectors are repressed, bulldozing their sovereignty, their cultures, and their relationship to the Earth. The ozone layer, the boreal forests, endangered species, are decimated. When the social commons are privatized, their accessibility diminishes, health, education deteriorate. When knowledge commons are patented, Indigenous and traditional ecological practices are forgotten. When cultural commons become merchandise, symbols, languages, and heritage are uprooted and disfigured.

Capitalism, the great culprit?

Some people point their finger at the "capitalocene," a concept that "signifies capitalism as a way of organizing nature—as a multispecies, situated, capitalist world-ecology [...] the basic historical pattern of modern world history as the "Age of Capital"—and the era of capitalism as a world-ecology of power, capital, and nature."[4] Here capitalism is an all-powerful, hegemonic, all-encompassing, system. A system to be torn down and replaced. Historically, and still today, despite differing positions on the State, this is the analysis put forth by a majority of Marxists and anarchists. The renowned thinker of social ecology, Mu ofy Bookchin, is no exception: social ecology aims to bring about a society that will have "eliminated not only capitalism but the Nation-State, not only classes but hierarchies, not only exploitation but domination, and, given that, will have constituted a rational and ecological alternative".[5]

For more than 10 years, I also believed this. Following Bookchin, I invested time and energy in local activism, fighting heart and soul, in Pointe-Saint-Charles and beyond, to change the world. In 2004, I founded *La Pointe libertaire* with Marcel Sévigny, an anarchist collective whose ideas and practices were inspired from social ecology and "aimed to stimulate self-organization in the neighbourhood and foster the (re)appropriation, by the collectivity, of all powers that concerns it."[6] In 2005, Marcel and I wrote:

> *"We are activists who were trained, for the one, in the autonomous community movement and municipal politics, and, for the other, in the radical feminist fringe of the anti-globalisation movement. Our different paths bring us to the same questions. What to do to challenge, in the long-term, multinational corporations' growing control over our collective heritage? How to go beyond a perpetual reaction to build a world without racism, sexism, poverty, and homophobia?"[7]*

Following Bookchin, we put ourselves to work to self-constitute a political community in our neighbourhood, in other words, to create decentralized and democratic political institutions. From this process, according to the theory, new "municipalities" would arise as the linchpin of direct democracy, and at their heart would be citizens' assemblies: "large general meetings in which all the citizens of a given area meet, deliberate, and make decisions on matters of common concern".[8]

Admittedly, we paid more attention to the political dimension of Bookchin's thought, libertarian municipalism, without worrying too much about the other dimension of his work, the social dimension. For Bookchin, the so-called social sphere, present in every culture, is of the private domain and includes, importantly, all of economic life. The goal of libertarian municipalism would be to municipalise the economy:

> *"A society organized along mutualistic, nonhierarchical, and communal lines would be most rational if it chose to replace the capitalist market economy with a moral economy,*

one whose members have a high sense of mutual obligation. It would replace classes and private property with coopera- tion and solidarity. It would replace profit with a recognition of mutual welfare. It would replace selling with sharing. It would replace rivalry and an illusory independence with re- ciprocity and interdependence. By replacing a profit-oriented economic nexus with an ethical one, it would transform the economy into culture."[9]

According to Bookchin, the city is the space for self-manage- ment and freedom. Outside of the (private) social sphere, freedom emerges when people meet in public spaces, when they share a civic life: from deliberation on common problems, the environment, educa- tion, the economy, the collective appreciation of public art, from the purchase and sale of goods and services, from socializing, from the exchange of information and news. Bookchin believes that:

"Only the community, however, is open to all adult mem- bers qua residents, not to workers and students alone, and can therefore become a broad arena for the management of communitywide affairs. [...] People would move from a state of being isolated monads to that of citizens who see them- selves in others, who are mutually dependent, and who, then, take responsibility for their common well-being."[10]

Municipal Libertarianism in Action

In real life though, the theory doesn't always apply, particularly when the majority of us haven't read Bookchin, except for one of the founding members of *La Pointe libertaire*: Marcel Sévigny, who was instrumental in helping the younger members of the collective discov- er this impressive body of work.[11] We nonetheless took action, follow- ing Bookchin's organizing method to a T. Once the political group was created (*La Pointe libertaire*), the objective was to promote the idea of the citizens' assembly by (self-)education, be it by organizing confer- ences, producing texts, engaging in direct action; in short, seize every opportunity to talk about the citizens' assembly. We published a whole slew of texts that we circulated in the neighbourhood and on our blog, that became, over time, an independent media fed by the *Agence de presse libre de la Pointe*: analyses of urban planning issues and strategies; a proposal for an ecovillage on the CN railyards; an analysis of the borough's municipal budget; a non-authorized biography of Vincent Chiara, a capitalist developer who bought the CN land for $1 (which earned us a notice for defamation!); on free public transit; a memoir on land development of the CN railyards; another on the struggles in the Indigenous community of Tyendinaga; another on racism and ethnic profiling; yet another on direct democracy; as well as a monthly critique of the borough's city council meetings.[12] We organised assemblies and workshops of all stripes: to discuss the film *Spezzano Albanese* on the political action of a libertarian collective in a small village in Italy; to elaborate on strategies to fight against the redevelopment of the Northern Electric factory into condos; to launch the self-managed Autonomous Social Center initiative; to discuss PARECON (participatory economy); to better understand gentrification, etc.

We also organised direct actions: we were able to force the CN to authorize the production of a community-led mural on the wall of its viaduct by starting it without asking for permission; similarly, the borough redesigned a notoriously dangerous bike path after our having issued an ultimatum—we gave them two weeks to fix it, threatening to otherwise pour concrete and install signage ourselves; we cleared the ragweed that had taken over a plot of land on the edge of the Lachine Canal to create the *Garden of Liberty*, today a space free from speculation because of its official recognition as a green space; we participated in the organisation of a squat in the old candle factory on the shores of the Lachine canal. We participated in the neighbourhood fight against the Casino's move to Pointe-Saint-Charles, against the conversion of the old Nordelec factory into condos, against the closure of the post office. We supported the struggle against the deportation of Abdelkader Belouani, notably by singing with him in his refugee sanctuary in the Saint-Gabriel Church; the anarchist choir of Point-Saint-Charles was born from this action and is now woven into the cultural fabric of the neighbourhood. We formed alliances with other anarchist groups in the South-West and, after many years of tension, with many of the grassroots community groups in the area. Other alliances were also forged, notably with the Convergence of Anticapitalist Struggles and Solidarity Against Borders and, as can be expected, we participated in a number of large anarchist gatherings, like the annual Anarchist Bookfair, and in protests, like the anticapitalist protests on

May 1st (in 2011 we organized the first Baby Bloc in Montréal[13]), the March 15th protests against police brutality, actions in support of Indigenous peoples' struggle, and the student strike in 2012. And, to complete the picture, we participated, hearts racing, in the Autonomous Popular Assembly (*l'assemblée populaire autonome de quartier*; APAQ) of Pointe-Saint-Charles. This assembly was born, as was the case for many other neighbourhoods, from the 2012 strike that was, at that point, no longer just a student strike, but a "people's" one. It was about time! We were approaching our Bookchinian vision of a self-managed political institution! But after a promising start and some interesting discussions about austerity, social housing, urban planning, and strategies of struggle, participation dwindled and the flame went out—the APAQ in our neighborhood disappeared.

It is not my intention here to do an evaluation of these 10 years of struggle But I do have an intuition to share. In retrospect, I call into question the starting-point of our organizing practice. For Bookchin, the starting-point is the political sphere. Eventually, the theory goes, a community, self-constituted into a libertarian "municipality" can decide to municipalize the economy or, in other words, to transform all the enterprises/organisations of the social sphere into public propriety.[14] My experience leads me to conclude that if, in Pointe-Saint-Charles—this dynamic, oppositional urban village, organized from the center to far-left—we have not, after 10 years of effort, succeeded in growing *La Pointe libertaire*, nor even have we constituted even the embryo of a political institution, it's that we have erred. This has led me to wonder what would happen if we took as a starting point not the political, but the socio-economic sphere.

Economy as Ecology

What would happen if we thought of the economy not as an objective category, but rather as a discursive product? If, instead of considering economic activity as an area of human activity separate from others, we thought of it as being of the social, the political, the ethical, the ecological?

"What if we were to see the economy as ecology—as a web of human ecological behaviors no longer bounded but fully integrated into a complex flow of ethical and energetic interdependencies: births, contaminations, self-organizings,

*mergings, extinctions, and patterns of habitat maintenance
and destruction? (...) How might we cultivate genuinely ethical ecological-economic sensibilities? How might we re-
configure our notions of economy and ecology in ways that
help us take responsibility for being alive together as life?"*[15]

This vision is the cornerstone of the Community Economies
Collective (CEC), based on J.K. Gibson-Graham's work,[16] that now
consists of more than 170 researchers around the world.[17] This collective seeks to bring about a political economy centered on the practice of self-determination, motivated by the idea that "another world is
possible" and aspiring towards post-capitalist futures.

J.K. Gibson-Graham and Ethan Miller propose three ways forward: rethinking being, rethinking the economy, and deliberating according to ethical coordinates to create *more-than-human* economies.[18]

Rethinking being (or existence). "Life does not exist without
community as a process of connection-amidst-difference, without being-in-common." (p.10) They invite us to put into question the idea
that *being-in-common*—that is to say community—is composed
uniquely of humans. They suggest rather that we broaden the spectrum
and conceive of multispecies communities, built on interrelated relationships of interdependence. This brings us to the second point: *rethinking the economy*: "Let us try to think 'economy' not as a unified
system or a domain of being but as diverse processes and interrela-
tions through which we (human and more-than-human) constitute
livelihoods." (p. 12). The economy (*oikos*—habitat; *nomos*—negotiation of order) could therefore be thought of as constituted of the diversity of subsistence activities within a community. Imagine then
diversified human economies coexisting, not only amongst themselves, but also with diverse economies of salmon, bees, bacteria, etc.,
as well as with larger community economies, communities that together, they produce and sustain. Ecology (*oikois*—habitat; *logos*—account of) thus becomes a way to understand the whole, or more
precisely, to see the aggregation of interactions of diverse economies.
"The ecological entry point forces us to step back from the temporary
centering operations of economics and ask how relations of livelihood
creation and collective provisioning interact, conflict, co-constitute
each other, and generate emergent properties." (p. 12)

We have redefined economy as ecology from the standpoint of actors constituting a community and producing livelihoods together, and ecology as the interactions of different diverse community economies. We arrive, then, at the ethical questions that lie at the heart of our economic and ecological relations: "How do we live together with human and non-human others?" (p. 14)

It's here that we find the idea of looking to identify spaces for ethical negotiation, or in other words, the *ethical coordinates*. Gibson-Graham and Miller suggest that an ethical stance for the Anthropocene demands that each person become skilled in negotiation: of participation, of necessity (or surviving well), of surplus (production, appropriation, distribution, and mobilisation), of commons.

If community is what emerges as living beings make and share worlds together, then community economies are the sites where we imagine and struggle—as increasingly-attentive members of a community of life—to balance our needs with the needs of others, to account for and to offer recompense for the gifts of surplus we receive from the earth and earth others, and to begin to build together an ethical practice of economy for living in—and beyond—the Anthropocene. (p. 15).

A Method of Organisation

For a community organiser like me, who is always interested in the application of theories and concepts, it is clear that we need to make this language more accessible. This is easier said than done:

While not theorized as such by Gibson-Graham, "community economy" can be read in her work as a polyvalent term that condenses three conceptually distinct, yet interrelated, moments. I will call these "CE1, "CE2," and "CE3". To summarize, CE1 is the "ontological moment" of community economy, an essentially negative and unfixable space characterized by a sharing of the very impossibility of fully capturing or mastering the nature of our being-together. CE2 is the "moment of ethical exposure", the affirmation of a demand to render visible and contestable the dynamics and consequences (and thus responsibilities) of our interrelationships. CE3 is, finally, the "moment of politics" in which the inevitable positivity of our collective ethical negotiations is made explicit and becomes a site of connection, exclusion, struggle, and active transformation.[19]

Let me try.

The construction of community economies (CE) is a continuous and non-linear process that is articulated in three key moments that we'll call here CE1, CE2, and CE3. To avoid ossification and exclusion (or the naturalisation), the process implies a constant back-and-forth (*va-et-vient*) between these different key moments. Each moment is animated by its openings, its closings, its tensions, its voids, its substance.

To start, in CE1, it's about working to put into question, to undo, to shake our certainties when it comes to the existence of one, fixed, common, community. To put into question our preconceived notions of what is "natural," of the unity or division of "our" collectivity. In other words, to take the time to examine this "us,"[20] to see its diversity, the differences that hide within it, the tensions that are at play.

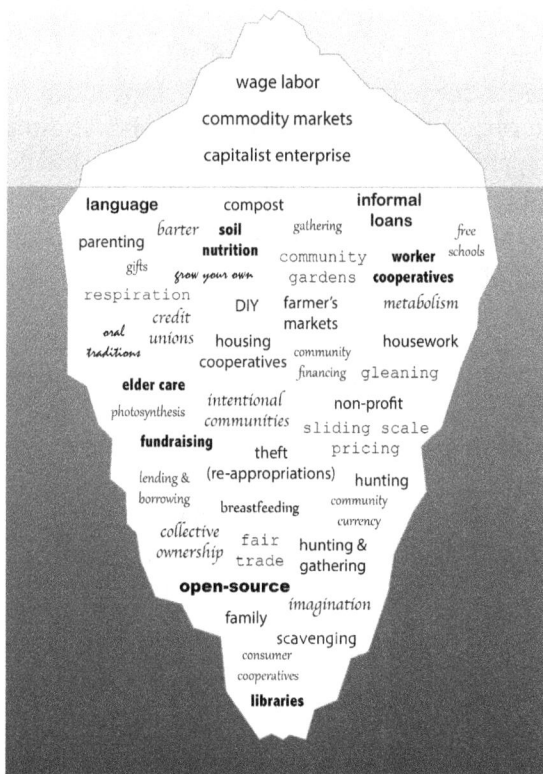

Figure 1. Source: Diverse Economies Iceberg by Community Economies Collective is licensed under a Creative Commons Attribution-Share Alike 4.0 International License.)

This process allows us to see what surrounds "us" with a(n always) fresh look, and in **CE2**, to perceive the diversity of activities that "we" perform that ensure "our" subsistence, "our" livelihoods.

Our job is thus to map what hides under the surface of the water (see figure 1), to name it, explain it, and value it. It would be, according to J.K. Gibson-Graham, a first step "toward imagining and enacting economic heterotopias—community economies in which well-being is produced directly".[21] To understand, together, that the economy is not in fact "a machine governed by immutable laws or mechanical principles."[22] In doing so, we eject capitalism, this all-powerful, hegemonic, system from the driver's seat. By broadening the economy, we see appear a multitude of ways to (re)appropriate it. Because these activities are familiar, intimate even. They are what make us live. They support us. We realize that we are the economy. We become economic subjects.

And here we are hit with a strange feeling.

If we are the economy, is it up to us to shape it? To create livelihoods that are not rooted in competition, each-for-their-own, greed? To put an end to oppression, to the exploitation of humans and the planet?

Here is the "political" moment (CE3), the moment of negotiation of livelihoods, of common subsistence, the meeting of individual and collective subjects that "seek to sustain and struggle for spaces in which interdependence is visible and collectively negotiated as they oppose processes of uncommoning or enclosure in all their forms,"[23] the (re)construction of self (the individual), and of us (the collective).[24] It is impossible, following to this school of thought, to know in advance what this livelihood will look like. This being-in-common emerges from deliberation, from tension, from struggles, from consensus, from tearing apart (and is transformed during this back-and-forth).

J.K. Gibson-Graham proposes ethical coordinates, as well as a series of tools,[25] to help us identify points of intervention. These tools permit us to understand that work is more complex than an activity to earn our bread and butter. Housework, in the community, on a volunteer basis or as mutual aid, is a facet of our lives that diversifies our experience and that contributes to satisfying different dimensions of our well-being (material, occupational, physical, social, and community). Following this same logic, our communities are supported by different types of enterprises/organisations. By increasing the diversity of enterprises/organisations, who direct their surplus toward the well-being of humans, communities, and our planet, we create a more viable future for everyone. Similarly, we meet our needs through encounters in markets, but also in other contexts within which we barter, offer gifts, or enter into relationships of mutual aid. By diversifying our encounters, our connections between each other and with the Earth are enriched and we become more apt to take care of one and other, especially in times of threat and scarcity. Next, the commons are not limited to one type of property; different types of property can be transformed into commons, that is to say, through the process in which a community takes responsibility for them and defines their use, access, and benefits. By enlarging the diversity of commons, we increase the chance that they are preserved and developed. Finally, it is also about leverage different forms of investment which subvert the logic of capitalist financing, in particular by the means of sweat equity and gifting, and to highlight, in our "financial" reports, rather than so-called economic degrowth, the growth of intact ecosystems, communities that share common goals and accumulated know-how.

This testifies to the fact that, like in nature, economic activity for one is intimately related to economic activity of another. And like in the natural world, economic change is path-dependent (that is, determined by observable preconditions) and capable of amazing deviations. The economy is not a solitary vessel that follows a predetermined path. Although we can adjust the helm to follow the course we have chosen, nothing guarantees we'll arrive at the port on time, or even at all. Currents, cyclones, mutinies, or refugee boats can make us change our course. Changing one element has an influence on the whole, as do unexpected events. All we can do is observe, adjust, and revise our actions in order to reach our goals.

There is therefore no model to perfect, no revolutionary moment or *Grand Soir* to anticipate, no rupture, no abolition of the system, no unique vision. Rather there is a broadening of the spectrum of emancipatory economic activities in a process of creation of community economies. Community economies are political spaces of ethical deliberation, of open process, both sensible and adaptable, that enable different communities to enact ways of being, of thinking and doing, to live their interdependence. None of this is static, because the challenges and preoccupations of one and other are diverse and change over time.

Back to Pointe-Saint-Charles

In Pointe-Saint-Charles, groups and individuals want to imagine, dream up, and experiment with "emancipatory" economic activities, activities that contribute to their subsistence, to better livelihoods. The activities/initiatives organised grassroots community organisations, anarchist groups, or a joyous mix of the two, abound: non-profit grocery stores, fruit and vegetable public markets, underground breweries, collective gardens, thrift stores, cafe-restaurants, alternative schools, maker-spaces. Bâtiment 7, an emergent "factory of collective autonomy," is a building that was expropriated from a capitalist developer[26] and today, chugs on quietly towards the creation of an autonomous and self-managed space organised around four poles: local services and collaborative workshops; family and health services; urban agriculture, and contemporary art.[27] And we must not forget to mention all those autonomous institutions, managed by neighbourhood folks, that take care of legal, advocacy, health, and education services; these historical commons that make Point-Saint-Charles a close-knit community that can buckle down and rise up when the situation demands it.[28]

From my perspective, it's already a community economy, albeit latent. It's waiting for us to make it visible, for folks to actively, intentionally, name and embrace it. Let us imagine CE1. CE1 is all those moments of meeting, formal or spontaneous, of conflict, of tension between different aspects of the neighbourhood (Working-class neighbourhood? Popular neighbourhood? Revitalised neighbourhood? Gentrified neighbourhood? A chauvinistic neighbourhood?) and their coexistence (Traditional population? *Bobos*? Young, middle-class families? Irish? French-Canadians? New immigrants? Kanien-keha:ke?). With this new look, let us imagine CE2.

CE2 are those moments we take to make visible all of the diversity of economic practices that already exist in Pointe-Saint-Charles. Imagine an assembly or a virtual participatory tool that would allow us to map all of the activities that are usually hidden, under the water. The initiatives listed above, but also all the whole *caring economy*, institutional or more organic, individual or collective (networks of families that trade-off child care; friends that are there for us when we have a crisis or need a shoulder to cry on; grand-parents who care for their sick grand-children when they can't go to school...). Or still, these transactions with others, these more or less formal networks of barter/exchange (tenants in collective housing recuperating bread, for example, and then redistributing it amongst their neighbours; children's clothing circulated from one family to the next; massage therapists and estheticians that exchange their services against a stay in the countryside). And, for example, all these forms of work that break with the logic of capitalism but contribute to the well-being of the population (volunteers who serve low-cost dinners on a daily basis in charitable organizations; health professionals who provide free services to the penniless; people who remove ragweed from a green space). Once this dimension is made visible, we get to CE3.

CE3 is the moment of deliberation, of radical democracy, of action as related to the diverse economy that has been made visible. What relations of interdependence emerge between humans, between humans and the more-than-human-world? What choices can we make, individually and collectively? How can we broaden the spectrum of economic practices that improve the life (survival) of everyone? And that of the planet? It is at this moment that we take stock of the obstacles. The rent is too high. Zoning is difficult to change. A capitalist supermarket has its eye on a local one. It is the moment to talk about power, domination, and influence. To understand together how capitalist activities hurt our neighbourhood. Even if the development of non-capitalist economic activities improves the well-being of individuals, communities, and the planet, we observe, for example, that the municipal council still has a tendency to legislate in favour of the interests of capital. However, groups of people constituted as community economies build their strength, their power to act in common, they establish alliances with other communities, temporary coalitions, or more permanent federations around specific issues, according to the needs of the moment. We can then conceive of the different territories as part of a vast set of spaces connected by a web of meaning, ideas, and practices that are propagated by everyday contact or by virtual networks. Remember, CE3 is never fixed, never definitive. The back-and-forth between CE1 and CE2, by way of CE3, is a revolutionary process by which individuals transform themselves, by which new subjectivities emerge; the individuals and the groups mutually transform themselves.

Last words

The political institution is not separate from the economy (the social). The point of departure is peoples' economic (social) activity in a given territory, this tangible, real, activity; from here emerge a politics. The political subjects are not "citizens', but wear all sorts of hats—gardener, mother, neighbour, municipal councillor, worker-owner, student, therapist. And these territories, constituted as community economies, create networks with community economies elsewhere, following the needs and desires of one and the other. The economy is diversified, not municipalized. Now, not "after." This allows us to see that we are not fighting against a global, abstract, capitalism, but against specific and visible capitalist activities. Education is not a preliminary step, but is rather done in action. In thinking and practicing the economy, we transform ourselves. Our way of imagining and talking about the economy influences our actions. Our actions create the economy. The economy, or in other words, ecology, this process of auto-constituting diverse communities, within which humans and more-than-humans interact to assure the subsistence and the livelihoods of each other, and of the generations to come.

Maybe you, reader, want to contribute to this thought process? You'd like to explore this method of organising? Don't hesitate. A better world will not be the fruits of someone else's labour. It is the fruit of our labour, right here, right now.

Endnotes

1 Because of my overly busy life, it is likely that this thought experiment would never have been made available to an English-speaking audience had Sean Devine not gifted of their precious time to its translation. I am truly grateful. This piece was originally published in French: "De l'écologie sociale aux économies de communauté: Pour un autre vivre-ensemble». In Collectif, V. Lefebvre-Faucher & M.A. Casselot (Eds.). *Faire partie du monde: Réflexions écoféministes* (pp. 53-73). Les éditions du remue-ménage, 2017.

2 K. Gibson, D. B. Rose et R. Fincher, «Preface», *Manifesto Manifesto for Living in the Anthropocene*, Brooklyn, Punctum Books, 2015, p vi.

3 The practices of enclosure and non-management are contrary to commoning. Enclosure restricts access and use of commons, while privatizing benefit and responsibility. When commons are not managed, access is far and wide, without restrictions, but, on the flip side, there is no community to take on responsibility and care.

4 J. W. Moore, «Introduction», dans J. W. Moore (dir.), *Anthropocene or Capitalocene?: Nature, History, and the Crisis of Capitalism*, Oakland, PM Press, 2016, p. 6.

5 J. Biehl, *Le municipalisme libertaire: La politique de l'écologie sociale*, Montréal, Écosociété, 1998, p. 20.

6 A. Kruzynski et M. Silvestro, «Proximité physique, vie de quartier et luttes anarchistes», dans R. Bellemare-Caron, É. Breton, M.-A. Cyr, F. Dupuis-Déri et A. Kruzynski (dir.), *Nous sommes ingouvernables: les anarchistes au Québec*, Montréal, Lux, 2013, p. 130.

7 A. Kruzynski et M. Sévigny, « Réhabiliter la politique : Une option libertaire », *Possibles*, vol. 29, no 1, 2005, p. 28-45.

8 Biehl, *Le municipalisme libertaire*, p. 102.

9 *Ibid.*, p. 211-212.

10 *Ibid.*, p. 99.

11 See M. Sévigny, *Trente ans de politique municipale: Plaidoyer pour une citoyenneté active*, Montréal, Écosociété, 2001 et M. Sévigny, *Et nous serions paresseux? Résistance populaire et autogestion libertaire*, Montréal, Écosociété, 2009.

12 See www.lapointelibertaire.org.

13 La Pointe libertaire, «Parents et enfants participent en grand nombre à la manifestation anticapitaliste du 1er mai!», communiqué de presse, 2011, http://archive.lapointelibertaire.org/node/1624.html, visited on June 20, 2017.

14 I doubt that a community could decide to municipalize the economy as a whole, without destroying itself in the process. Imagine that this decision is not unanimous, but adopted by majority. If the libertarian "municipality" chose to do it anyway, does this not represent an authoritarian act?

15 J. K. Gibson-Graham et E. Miller, «Economy as Ecological Livelihood», in Katherine Gibson, Deborah Bird Rose et Ruth Fincher (dir.), *Manifesto for Living in the Anthropocene*, Brooklyn, Punctum Books, 2015, p. 8.

16 J.K. Gibson-Graham is the penname for Julie Graham and Katherine Gibson, feminist geographers specialising in political economy. Their theoretical and empirical body of work is immense.

17 Surprise! Cisgender white men are not the majority as is often the case in the field of economics.

18 These explanations come from a free-mix and paraphrasing of ideas present in Gibson-Graham and Miller's "Economy as Ecological Livelihood".

19 E. Miller, «Community Economy: Ontology, Ethics and Politics for Radically Democratic Economic Organizing», *Rethinking Marxism*, vol. 25, no 4, 2013, p. 519-520.

20 I put the "us" in quotation marks to signify that there is no united and homogenous "us', but rather many diversified "I"s that come together.

21 J. K. Gibson-Graham, «Being the Revolution, or, How to Live in a "More-Than-Capitalist" World Threatened with Extinction», *Rethinking Marxism*, vol. 26, no 1, 2014, p.81.

22 J. K. Gibson-Graham, J. Cameron et S. Healy, *Take Back the Economy: An Ethical Guide for Transforming Communities*, Minneapolis, University of Minnesota Press, 2013, p. 189.

23 Miller, «Community Economy...», p. 526.

24 J. K. Gibson-Graham, *A Postcapitalist Politics*, Minneapolis, University of Minnesota Press, 2006, p. x.

25 See http://communityeconomies.org/

26 This history is recounted in the book, produced by *La Pointe liberaire : Bâtiment 7: Victoire populaire à Pointe-Saint-Charles*, Montréal, Écosociété, 2013.

27 A. Kruzynski, L'autonomie collective en action: du Centre Social Autogéré de Pointe-Saint-Charles au Bâtiment 7, *Nouvelles pratiques sociales, L'action communautaire: Quelle autonomie? Pour qui?*, 29(1), 2017, pp. 139-158.

28 Kruzynski, A. Commoning property in the City: the on-going work of making and remaking. In Kelly Dombroski & J.K. Gibson-Graham, *Handbook of Diverse Economies*, Edward Elgar Publishing, in press. ; Collectif CourtePointe (Isabelle Drolet et Anna Kruzynski (dir.), *Pointe Saint-Charles: un quartier, des femmes, une histoire communautaire*, Montréal, Remue-ménage, 2006; K. Triollet, «Une décennie de luttes urbaines à Pointe-Saint-Charles: Vers une réappropriation citoyenne», *Nouveaux Cahiers du socialisme*, no 10, *Occupons la ville!*, 2013, p. 129-143.

Annex

The FRAP Manifesto

Translated by Sean Devine, Symbiosis Montréal

I
The Sense in Our Action

I
Why engage in political action

Workers[1] are excluded from power

In Montréal, workers are often excluded or absent from the decision-making process, be it in municipal councils, school boards, public office (like the *Regie du logement*[2]), and even in caisse populaires.[3] It is the bourgeoisie—who represent only a minority in comparison to the rest of the population—that occupy most positions of power.

This lack of power costs workers dearly

The absence of workers in important decision-making positions comes at a great cost. What workers win through organisation (negotiations, strikes, pressures on bosses, etc.), they lose on the political landscape when their taxes are raised or their social benefits are compromised. And so the elimination of real-estate speculation, the construction of affordable housing, the protection of non-unionized workers, accessible health care, or control of commercial business remain out of their control.

A popular movement is on the rise

Faced with this absence of workers in decision-making positions, a social movement is rising. Citizen committees and tenants' associations have sprung up in many neighbourhoods across Montréal. Some unions have shifted direction to become more engaged on the political front. Students protest. In short, regular people—workers or not—are charging into a fight that is only just starting. This fight is diverse, but increasingly brings us to the following conclusion: **it is necessary to engage in political action as soon as possible to change the balance of power. Otherwise, we are at a dead end.**

II
Who to attack

The Drapeau-Saulnier Group

The Drapeau-Saulnier group[4] does not represent power for the people. They are the embodiment of big-city capitalism expressed at the municipal level in Montréal.

• There are a host of **influential economic bodies** who have direct or indirect ties to municipal politics. The private sector can be found everywhere: in recreation and culture (Expo67 and the baseball stadium are the obvious examples), in housing that's left in the hands of speculators, in "trusts" and professionals, in transportation (from which, for example, Murray Hill has been profiting for years now),[5] in information, for which most of it in Montréal is concentrated and controlled by the "Power Corporation's" Desmarais group.

• Municipal government is composed almost entirely of a class of **powerful leaders.** Of the 52 members of the municipal council, 50 members—or 96%— are professionals or businessmen.

• What's more, we can take a look at the City of Montréal's budget to see where their priorities really lie: the Expo, Place des Arts, the baseball stadium, the Olympic games... and only 1000 housing units (constructed in the last 10 years), whereas we would need at least 7500/year.

In short, behind the façade, behind Drapeau-Saulnier's appearance of prestige, seriousness, and efficiency, we find private interests, the market, and privilege.

This is why we must focus our attack on municipal power.

Private industry

We must also attack private industry. Those that say the solution to worker's woes in Montréal is to be found in the private sector are sorely mistaken.

It is our belief that the solution will never be found in private industry or organised capitalism, but in the political organisation of workers who will see to it that the economy is run with the needs of the population in mind, and not as a function of the interests of Anglo-Candian, American, or Franco-Canadian capitalists.

For us, this means that a municipal political movement is opposed to the current municipal government and the team that heads it.

III
Building popular power

Municipal power

We will operate out of Montréal, because it is Quebec's social and economic core. It comprises around half of Quebec's population and, as a consequence, any political action that happens in Montréal will ripple throughout all of Quebec.

Our main target is municipal power, because it constitutes one of the major causes of our situation and acts as a springboard for effective organisation.

It is important to note however that this is but a **first step.** Municipal power represents only a first victory in the battle, allowing workers to gain real political power, which they currently lack at both the municipal and national level, be it with the *Union Nationale* or the Liberal Party.[6]

Where our action is headed

We no longer want to be relegated to the role of watchdog of the powerful, we want to be those who **exercise the power.**

As such, we must create the conditions that make this situation favourable for:

• The creation of a new radical municipalist party;

• Autonomy from powerful economic groups and private industry;

• The benefit of the workers; that is to say in the interest of the majority of the population and of collective political participation for all workers.

Organising our battle

In the current situation, there are three groups that are fighting in different, but parallel ways: **non-unionized workers**—the unemployed, those on welfare—**unionized workers**—blue collar, white-collar, and technicians—and **students,** as well as the young in general.

The manifold actions carried out by these groups rarely coalesce. This is why it is necessary to coordinate these diverse movements aiming to improve housing, transport, well-being, education, etc. into collective action at the political level by building a political organisation that unites non-unionized workers, unionized workers, consumers, students, and tenants around common goals.

In other words, we must build popular power for workers beyond the existing parties at the municipal level.

As such, it is necessary to create political action committees in every neighbourhood in Montréal, based on electoral districts, and to form a collective political front that spans the whole city.

II
Political Action Committees

The Political Action Committee (PAC) is the Front D'action Politique's (FRAP) basic unit. It acts as both a rallying point and a base of operations for the FRAP in every electoral district of Montréal.

I
What is the PAC?

PACs' goals

The ultimate aim of the PAC is to create a society built by workers based on the priorities that are important to them. Reaching this ultimate objective requires fulfilling the following three goals:

• Establishing a true urban democracy in Montréal, based on worker participation in the decision-making process at every level;

• Providing the opportunity to participate in political life in Montréal to the largest number of workers possible;

• Fostering unity among all workers in Montréal, whether they are unionized, non-unionized, unemployed or recipients of welfare, tenants, or students.

First note: These three goals presuppose the abolition of capitalism as it currently exists at the municipal level—or at least, to deliver it a serious blow.

At the same time, it means we must state what we really believe to be the ideal society. We want a participative democracy; that is to say, we want more than one vote every four years and a brief presented to the government. We want workers to have **real weight when it comes to the decisions that are made**, so they can have real choice (for instance, to choose between a permanent Exposition or the construction of housing).

Second note: We are not talking here about the participation offered by the powers that be, but participation that will be made possible by a political organization of workers.

We reject means of participation that serve only to better control us or that keep us from being free from the current powers, such as parliamentary commissions or the housing committee, where three citizens that represent no one speak for the entire population of Montréal, and so on.

Consequently, **our current—and future—participation will foremost take the form of struggles** that we organize on different fronts.

Fighting on three fronts

Political Action Committees are mobilized units that must fight on many fronts at the same time, given that the interests of the working class are not limited to just one area.

• **Consumption.** We must organize as a function of our immediate needs, such as housing, health, food, credit, etc. In this regard, co-operatives are a weapon that allow us to begin organizing popular power. Therefore, workers must take control of the *caisses populaires*, form cooperatives, etc.

• **Work.** The consolidation of a true solidarity among workers remains of critical importance. Workers' struggles for better wages and better working conditions must be broadened and aim for the establishment of workers' power in factories and businesses. On the labour front, militants from the Political Action Committee will support union and working class struggles by educating the public on workers' issues and by organizing solidarity between citizens and workers.

• **Municipal politics.** On this front, we must channel the energy from popular (citizen) groups and use it to organise a political plan at the municipal level in order to orient the political towards the will of the majority. We must, for instance, carefully watch municipal councillors, organize public assemblies to confront them, and, when our collective force allows for it, present candidates to represent electoral districts.

Basic principles

1. The PAC is the basic political unit for the general working class movement in Montréal.

2. The PAC is united with every popular neighbourhood organization (citizens committees, tenants associates, student groups, etc.) and with every popular organization within the private sector (unions, workers committees, etc.).

3. The PAC bases its actions at the level of the electoral district.

4. All actions and positions taken by a PAC that directly involve the movement as a whole (that is, every other PAC) must be brought to the attention of the permanent council or to the general assembly. That being said, each PAC is independent within their district for all that is relevant to their district.

5. All electoral struggles will be subordinate to the people's struggles. This way, the election of a candidate to the municipal council is not a goal in-and-of-itself, but a way to frame popular struggles. The central goal of the PAC is to offer unwavering support to all popular struggles, whether they be the control of the *caisses populaires*, the creation of cooperatives, and so on. As such, electoral struggles are but one aspect of our work, whose significance can only be derived from the totality of struggles it is part of.

Who are the members of a PAC?

Any worker can be part of a PAC. That is:

• **Workers**, whether they be unionized or not, as well as the unemployed or welfare-recipients, who are, in point of fact, workers by right;

• **Students**, who we consider as future workers, since they will one day have to work for employers themselves;

• **Intellectual-workers**, such as professors, researchers, technicians, etc.

II
What does a PAC do?

A PAC's role

6. Help **coordinate** existing struggles and regroup popular organisations together.

7. **Politicise** the population by showing them that the real causes of their problems stem from their political situation. To do this:

• We inform workers on their rights and ways they can take power;

• We systematically denounce situations of injustice caused by misused political power or private industry;

• We provide unwavering support to workers' struggles taken up by one or many citizens;

Our Priorities

• **In the short term, our priorities are:**

– To organise a PAC in each district, started by determined political militants;

– Determine the most important problems that we must tackle first;

– Establish an action plan, based on each district;

– Build an efficient information system within each district (community centre, parishes, *caisses populaires*, any type of association, etc.)

– Recruit and train militants.

• **In the medium-term, we must:**

– Stimulate collective interest in the greatest number of citizens as possible (example: support the extension of the cooperative movement);

– Take control of the instruments of popular promotion (e.g., *caisses populaires*)

– Systematically organise cadicacy campaigns to municipal councils;

– Foster the creation of bodies of political actions in workplaces and schools.

• In the long-term:

We want to establish a real urban democracy that is decentralised and based on local electoral districts, as well as promote direct democracy within the government and workplace.

On the Note of Candidacy:

The following rules are put in place:

8. We must totally dissociate ourselves from the traditional elites by refusing all support coming from non-workers. Experience demonstrates that entrepreneurs, "independent" professionals, and other members of the bourgeoisie will support a "working-class" candidate only to buy them and gain better control. It is critical that we avoid this situation.

9. Before any foray into electoral politics, we must have structured PACs in at least 6 or 7 districts across Montréal.

10. PACs will finance their own campaign in their district (excluding financial support coming from other PACs or from the permanent council).

11. The general assembly of the FRAP will decide if a candidate will be put up for election, as well in which district the candidate will run.

12. Candidates are elected within each PAC and the general assembly of the FRAP must ratify the running of a candidate elected by the PAC.

13. Candidates do not run as individuals, but as a candidate of the FRAP As such, the general assembly of the FRAP can recall an elected candidate's mandate at any time if it is judged that they are not working towards the objectives of the movement.

As a mobile unit, the PAC has great autonomy.

It is important to remember however that the fight must take place across all of Montréal and that it will only be able to replace the powers that be when the PACs constitute a true common front across the whole city and that the fight exists within the framework of all working-class movements across Quebec.

III

THE FRONT D'ACTION POLITIQUE FRAP

The FRAP is a regrouping of PACs in each district across Montréal, as well as representatives from popular organisations who share in the goals and objectives set forth by the PACs. It is by the FRAP that we organise the coordination of struggles across Montréal.

Structure of the FRAP

General Assembly

The general assembly is composed of all members of each PAC, as well as representatives of popular organisations that subscribed to the goals set out by the general assembly.

The general assembly gathers once a month to decide the priority of actions. It is sovereign in all domains.

Permanent Council

• **Role:** The permanent council is charged with overwatching the execution of decisions taken by the general assembly and making decisions that must be taken between general assembly meetings. It must therefore make sure that:

– The movement is properly represented according to popular opinion

– The movement maintains a continued link with all groups and popular organisations across Montréal

– The PACs have adequate technical assistance when necessary.

• **Composition:** It is composed of:
Two delegates elected by each PAC
  – A representative from each popular organisation that adheres to the FRAP
  – Five members elected by the secretariat

Secretariat
• **Its Role:** It is the executive branch of the movement. It is charged with the administration of the day-to-day. That is, it executes the tasks decided upon by the permanent council.
• **Composition:** Five members elected by the general assembly:
  – One responsible for organization
  – One responsible for training
  – One responsible for research and documentation
  – One responsible for external affairs
  – **One responsible for general coordination (secretary and information-keeping).**

Endnotes

1 Translator's Note (TN): I chose to translate the term "salariés" as "worker". This might sound of a Marxist ring to some readers, but given the time the FRAP Manifesto was written and the use of the word throughout, I felt as though it was the best, most encompassing, option. The direct translation would be "the salaried" or the "salaried workers". For those averse to this type of talk, another—I think clunkier—phrase might be "waged labourers", though, as we will see, the "waged" part of this phrase is not necessarily determinant for the definition of the term.

2 Quebec's Housing Board.

3 TN: A possible translation for caisses populaires could be "credit unions". I left it in its original French for two reasons: (a) a caisse populaire is not exactly identical to a credit union (though they are quite similar) and (b) the term caisse populaire has cultural significance to Quebecers, in such a way that the term "credit union" would lessen some of the impact of the statements made throughout the Manifesto.

4 TN: Lucien Saulnier and Jean Drapeau formed a fierce political duo in 1960's Quebec. Together they founded Quebec's Civic Party (Parti Civique or Civic Action League). During part of the time Drapeau was the mayor of Montréal, Saulnier acted as the chair of the executive committee and was head of the Montréal Urban Community. Their administration oversaw a number of projects in Montréal that the FRAP strongly criticized, some of which are mentioned in this document (the baseball stadium, Place Des Arts, etc.).

5 TN: Murray Hill is a private bus charter in Quebec. They had struck a deal with the city that made them the sole transporter for passengers traveling from the popular Dorval Airport - the nearest airport to Montréal's downtown core. This deal proved massively profitable for the company. Their monopoly was lost after, taxi drivers in 1969 surrounded Murray-Hill's garage in Griffintown (a burough of Montréal) during what has come to be known as the Murray-Hill Riot.

6 TN: The Union Nationale was a conservative and nationalist provincial party in Quebec. They won a majority government in 1966. The Liberal Party is a liberal federal party in Canada who, during the time of the FRAP, had either a majority or minority government.

About the contributors

Brian Tokar is an activist and author, a Lecturer in Environmental Studies at the University of Vermont, and a board member of the Institute for Social Ecology and 350Vermont.

Robert Kaminskiis an organizer with the Seattle Neighborhood Action Coalition.

Peter Marcuse is a Professor Emeritus of Urban Planning at Columbia University.

Margit Mayer is a Professor in the Department of Political Science at Freie Universität Berlin.

David Harvey is a Distinguished Professor of Anthropology at the CUNY Graduate Center.

Veronika Duma is a historian and a Research Associate at the Chair for Research on the History and Impact of the Holocaust at the Goethe University Frankfurt am Main.

Hanna Lichtenberger is a political scientist and historian in the Department of Political Science at the University of Vienna.

Donald Cuccioletta is a member of the Montréal Urban Left, a Founding Member of the FRAP, and a Coordinator for Nouveaux cahiers du Socialisme.

Nazan Üstündağ is an Academy in Exile and IIE-Scholar Rescue Fund Fellow at the Forum Transregionale Studien.

Barucha Peller is a writer and photographer based in California.

Jonathan Durand Folco is an Assistant Professor at the School of Social Innovation at Saint Paul University.

Jonny Gordon-Farleigh is the co-founder of Stir to Action, a co-operative building a new economy through democratic ownership and an editor of Stir magazine.

Kali Akuno is the co-founder and executive director of Cooperation Jackson.

Antje Dieterich is a PhD candidate at the Latin American Studies Institute, Free University Berlin.

Austin Krauss is an activist and artist based in New York.

Anna Kruzynski is a professor at the School of Community and Public Affairs and director of the Community Economy Development program at Concordia University.

Jason Toney is an activist, researcher and publisher based in Montreal.

More about Cities from Black Rose Books

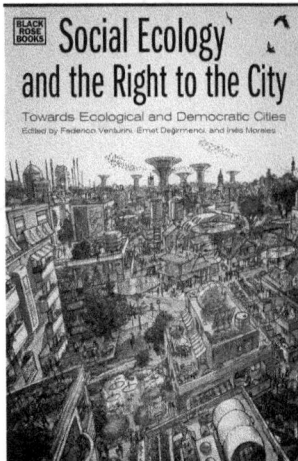

Social Ecology and the Right to the City

Social Ecology and the Right to the City
Towards Ecological and Democratic Cities
Edited by Federico Venturini, Emet Değirmenci, and Inés Morales

Paperback: 9781551646817
Cloth: 9781551646831
Ebook: 9781551646855

Advancing Urban Rights

ADVANCING URBAN RIGHTS
EQUALITY AND DIVERSITY IN THE CITY
EVA GARCIA-CHUECA, LORENZO VIDAL, EDS

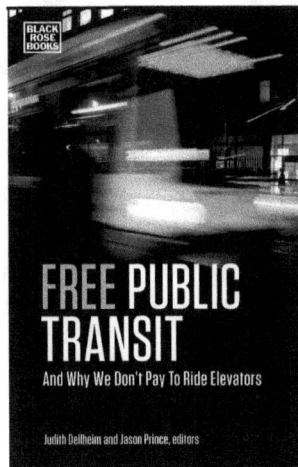

Advancing Urban Rights

Paperback: 9781551647678
Cloth: 9781551647692
Ebook: 9781551647715

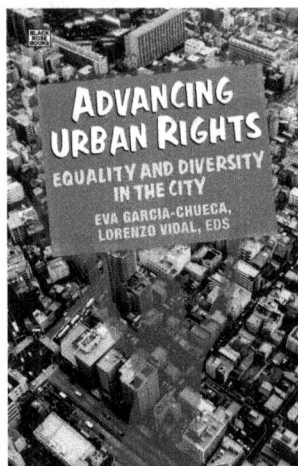

Free Public Transit

Paperback: 9781551646572
Cloth: 9781551646596
Ebook: 9781551646619

FREE PUBLIC TRANSIT
And Why We Don't Pay To Ride Elevators
Judith Dellheim and Jason Prince, editors

Transformative Planning

TRANSFORMATIVE PLANNING
RADICAL ALTERNATIVES TO NEOLIBERAL URBANISM
EDITED BY TOM ANGOTTI

Transformative Planning

Paperback: 9781551646916
Cloth: 9781551646930
Ebook: 9781551646954